The Follies of King Edward VII

The Follies of King Edward VII

Allen Andrews

LEXINGTON

Published in 1975 by:

LEXINGTON PRESS LIMITED,
28, Lexington Street,
London, W1R 3HR.
England

NCH: PB 205961
EDW

Designed by Bridget Heal
Picture Research by Shelia Rock

ISBN 0 904312 15 1

Printed by Tinling (1973) Limited, Prescot, Merseyside
(a member of the Oxley Printing Group Ltd)

TO JOYCE,

the ultimate folly.

('Folly is the direct pursuit of Happiness and Beauty.'
Shaw, *Maxims for Revolutionists.)*

Contents

Tea
and
Sympathy

king is not allowed the luxury of a good character, as Shaw's King Magnus remarked with deep feeling, observing that our country has produced millions of blameless greengrocers, but not one blameless monarch. After the modern intrusion of the candid television camera, we are now ruefully aware that even the private life of greengrocers can be of the earth, earthy as unwashed King Edwards. But, on balance, the cushioned palace is still a more reliable house of ill fame than the open-fronted shop.

Ill fame may not, of course, be the direct result of folly, and need not even be justifiably earned. What prudes call folly may be only the voice of envy deriding other men's courage. Yet the friends of King Edward the Seventh testified unreservedly to the width and depth of his aberrations, while claiming that they only strengthened affection for him. 'How *human* he was!' said Admiral of the Fleet Lord (Jacky) Fisher after the King's death. 'He could sin, "as it were with a cart-rope", and yet could be loved the more for it!'

Alongside his sins there were relative foibles, although most of them find a place among the Seven Deadlies. He was so superstitious that he would never allow his valet to turn his mattress on a Friday, never sat down thirteen at table unless one of the ladies present were pregnant—a matter over which he had, of course, a certain control. He was gargantuan in his appetite, habitually consuming twelve-course dinners. He was meticulously concerned with costume and uniform, and took a childish delight in dressing up in appropriate selections from the largest military wardrobe in the world, which filled the top floor of his residence—besides being Admiral of the Fleet, a Field-Marshal, and Colonel of several regiments, he held honorary rank in the military and naval forces of all the monarchies of Europe, and his headgear (size seven and one-eighth) included fifty different helmets and cocked hats, and earned him the nickname 'Old Peacock' from his nephew Willy, Kaiser Wilhelm of the German Empire. He gambled more heavily on cards and horses than his creditors thought suitable to their own stability, until a long last burst of racing successes brought him in an average profit of £25,000 a year.

But, above all, Edward formularized seduction into a pattern almost as rigid as court etiquette. It was as if he were living in a completely different era from his consort Alexandra or his mother, Queen Victoria. Alexandra floated back eight centuries to play out the idealised role of the queen of courtly love in old Romance, whom her troubadours were permitted to worship but never to touch. Edward, as Prince of Wales and king, merely jumped five centuries back and three to the side, like a chess-knight, or a toad.

Admiral of the Fleet Lord (Jacky) Fisher, seen here in his fifties before his appointment as First Sea Lord, loved Edward for his follies as well as for the determined opposition to German naval domination which they shared. Edward, right, the man with fifty uniforms, plays the Gay Hussar as Colonel of the Tenth (Hussars).

A DERBY FAVOURITE.

Sir John Tenniel, the illustrator of *Alice* who made his reputation with a 50-year career as a *Punch* cartoonist, tipped a winner with this loyal greeting, published on Derby Day 1896. Edward's horse won.

Newmarket, 1885. Edward moved his horses from Kingsclere to Richard Marsh's stables at Newmarket later, but he had permanent private quarters within the Jockey Club at Newmarket.

He exercised the equivalent of a *droit de seigneur* which only differed from the feudal practice in that he preferred the matured and sophisticated wives of the British aristocracy, with complaisant husbands cohabitant and living, rather than the mediaeval roster of peasant virgins. In spite of the unreliable contraceptive methods of the day he sired no blatant bastards, even if the cadet ranks of the nobility were swollen with demi-royal immigrants, whose descendants, like those of Nell Gwynne, are now sufficiently removed from the censure of those times to begin to boast about their origin.

Edward did not fall naturally into this pattern of seduction, but evolved the routine of appeasement of his carnal appetites fairly fast after a preliminary diet of actresses. There are only two broad exceptions to this generalization. Fourteen years after his marriage,

Edward responded to the doubling intensity of his seven-year-itch by making a determined assault on no less than three debutantes. This excited the public comment within Society: 'Why is the Prince no longer concerned with married ladies?' It also prompted private comment within Marlborough House, the huge square mansion opposite St James's Palace which was the residence of the Prince and Princess of Wales. One of the girls concerned was an American named Miss Chamberlayne, whom Alexandra consistently referred to as Miss Chamberpots.

This, regrettably, was not below the general standard of humour of the time and place. Alexandra was lively but not bright. Very shortly afterwards, she went to Athens to stay with her brother, King George of Greece (grandfather of the present Duke of Edinburgh). Then Edward made Mrs Lillie Langtry, 'the Jersey lily', his first official mistress—'official' in the sense that Alexandra later accepted the situation, even entertaining Mrs Langtry at Marlborough House, and therefore Society accepted it, though never Queen Victoria.

Lillie's reign as Edward's mistress marked a transition. He now abandoned actresses except for casual copulation, and began to dent the couches of Society ladies already established as the mothers of an unchallenged brood. Thirty years later there may have been another stage which is less well documented. Frank Harris

prints a depressing story of King Edward requesting from one of his mistresses, and being granted, permission to fumble her thirteen-year-old daughter. It is not entirely incredible of a sixty-five-year-old who had, all through his private life, been given everything he asked for. But the bohemian Frank Harris, though he was editor of three important literary and political reviews and was undoubtedly one of King Edward's raffish acquaintances, is always suspect as a social historian, if only because Society could never tolerate him for long enough at a time to enable him to penetrate very far into their private lives. As his friend Oscar Wilde, to whom he was intermittently generous after Wilde's downfall, said of him, 'Frank Harris is invited to all the great houses in England—once.'

There is no doubt that Edward the Seventh exercised a strange charm which earned him almost instant forgiveness from the majority of the British. He managed to enthrall influential public opinion with the understanding that the ladies he dallied with gave

'After Ascot — A Quiet Fizz Dinner' is the title of this social record of 1893. Edward used to end the Ascot festivities at a Ladies' Night with the Household Brigade.

'Tum-Tum', A swell in every sense of the word. Even in a studio the diminutive Edward needs a rock under his foot to be comfortable on the property parapet.

him their all, not only willingly, but so ardently that Edward would have been no gentleman if he had declined. Even *The Times,* when the King ascended the throne, commented with unctuous charity that the Monarch had in the past been importuned by allurement in its most seductive forms, so that his prayer 'Lead us not into temptation' must often have been uttered 'with a feeling akin to hopelessness.' Condonement could hardly go farther.

Much of Edward's dalliance was effected in the drawing-room, after luncheon or punctuated by five-o'clock tea. And it was the sofas of his favourites which took a deal of punishment, as did the favourites themselves. For the Prince was a heavy man: at the height of his desire, if not his performance, he was forty-eight inches round the belly and the same round the chest, and was known to his friends affectionately as 'Tum-Tum'.

The practice developed that husbands in high society should rarely come home for lunch and never for tea, with an underlined and reiterated *not, repeat not* if Edward was interested in their wives. The evidence is that this convention was established only because Edward, as sovereign of Society for thirty-five years before he became king, favoured it and cultivated it and reserved it for himself alone. Edward, in fact, extended licensed seduction hours from the period around supper-time, which was observed when he was a young man, to the full twelve hours following one-o'clock luncheon, the period which was in force—for Edward only—at the peak of his career.

He also broadened the venue, which was no longer restricted to private dining-rooms above Kettner's Restaurant in Romilly Street, Soho, or Rule's in the ineptly named Maiden Lane in Covent Garden. Ladies of distinction could now be tupped in their own drawing-room, and therefore in something approaching full after-noon dress. In the absence of *déshabillé*, this naturally led to con-siderable disarray. Lillie Langtry was famous for *not* lacing herself in with stays, but few other ladies had either the courage or the figure to follow this lead, but at some juncture some sort of ease-ment would be necessary.

A further difficulty was the inadequate capacity of the sofa. (A minor tragedy for Victorian lovers is indicated by the fact that the roomier chesterfield is not noted by the Oxford English Dictionary as a word used before 1900.) What with the narrow gauge of the sofa and the manipulation of some two yards of corset-lacing, there were certain difficulties about daytime seduction. They were overcome, though at great inconvenience. As the actress Mrs Pat Campbell, who had had her share of dressing-room and drawing-

Edward raced *Britannia* to gain nautical prestige for Great Britain against Kaiser Wilhelm of Germany, who even used Cowes Regatta to boost the reputation of the German Navy.

room adventures, observed with infinite relief when she finally married again, 'Ah, the deep, deep bliss of the double bed, after the hurly-burly of the chaise longue!'

The double bed was not, of course, unknown to Edward, apart from its marital use. As Prince of Wales and king he slept in more beds than most of his subjects. In an average year, and his annual routine was quite firmly fixed, Edward spent four months at Marlborough House in London; two months at Sandringham, Norfolk; one month at Abergeldie, his Scottish seat near Balmoral; six weeks as a guest at country house-parties given all over Britain; three weeks' yachting at Cowes followed by five weeks' diversion in France; and six weeks at a German spa getting his weight down and his dangle up. For at least a third of the year he was physically absent from Alexandra, and for much of the rest of the time he was out of her control. The Edwardian country-house parties have earned the widest notoriety as the assignation houses of the rich, where ingenious hostesses, having participated in or connived at the despatch of footloose husbands to distant grouse-moors, invited the relevant wife and her current lover, and puzzled over how to position the bedrooms. Next door was too obvious, the next floor was too far, with not even the excuse of the water-closet as alibi for the midnight hunter spotted and effusively and maliciously hailed in the wrong corridor.

But it was not only at the country-house parties of others that Edward was discreetly accommodated in this way. The same complicated put-and-take was carried out when he was the host. Sandringham was his own country home, and he and Alexandra entertained continuously. The stars of the company were accorded special arrangements for travel and reception. They would catch 'the Prince's train', a special, running on Saturday afternoons from London to Wolverton, where Edward had built a private railway station two miles from his home, and installed a luxury suite of lounges and powder-rooms. A fleet of horse-carriages and luggage-brakes conveyed the guests to Sandringham, where they were installed in apartments the allocation of which Edward—not Alexandra— had determined with great care. Alexandra was allowed to help place the guests at the dinner table. There was room for twenty-four at an oblong dining-table where the hosts sat opposite each other in the middle, not at the end. Because Sandringham was considered Edward's private house even when he was king, as opposed to the State residences of Buckingham Palace and Windsor Castle, he permitted himself the privilege of pursuing his private affairs even under his wife's roof. And it is not strictly true, in spite of the assiduously leaked reports of her complaisance, that Alexandra liked the set-up, although perforce she tolerated it. She was known to explode in derisive laughter at the sight of King Edward and Mrs Alice Keppel, the last and most indulged of Edward's steady mistresses, driving past her windows at Sandringham portraying the excessive domestic bliss of Darby and Joan on an afternoon jaunt.

Sandringham House, Norfolk, bought as a private residence for Edward and Alexandra on their wedding at a price of £220,000 with 7000 acres, was formerly the property of a gentleman who chose to live abroad after marrying his mistress.

Shooting at Lambton Castle, the home of the Earl of Durham. Edward bags one for the pot. For the one man in the firing line there are seven in reserve.

For many years while he was Prince of Wales, Edward's principal pimp and procurer was Harry Tyrwhitt-Wilson, known to his circle as 'the Smiler'. He was both the Prince's equerry and an intimate friend of Lord Randolph Churchill, Winston's father. This was a dual loyalty which was strongly tested when Edward ostracized Churchill, and anyone who entertained him, for eight years after the Aylesford scandal (see Chapter VI). Since Edward had an arbitrary way of inviting himself to house-parties, it was Tyrwhitt-Wilson's delicate task to indicate to a host and hostess that the Prince would like to pay a visit, and, further, he submitted a list of fellow-guests 'who are likely to be approved'.

Tyrwhitt-Wilson also arranged the London seductions, timed for after lunch or afternoon tea. It was he who codified in black and white the husband-excluding technique introduced by Edward. The

Smiler carried a message to the favoured lady in the morning, revealing that the Prince intended to call, and delineated the new model of manners: 'It is etiquette that the person called on shall receive no other visitors and that no other member of the family shall be present during the visit, unless inquired for by the Prince.'

Tyrwhitt-Wilson occasionally lent his own house to Edward as a place of assignation, and on one occasion at least the arrangement went wildly awry. Edward was conducting an affair with 'a lady of title' (a Victorian phrase which irresistibly recalls the alleged title of a contemporary volume of memoirs, *My Life Under Five Sovereigns,* by A Lady Of Title). It was agreed that the lady should meet the Prince at Tyrwhitt-Wilson's house after the opera. She drove up in a hansom-cab and found Edward vainly fishing in the gutter. He had dropped the Smiler's door-key down the street drain and could not retrieve it. The lady suggested that, since they could not go inside, they might at least take some comfort by driving around London in the closed cab. They did so, and the Prince finally took

her to her home, paying off the cabbie with a shilling, which, in his inexperience, he thought was the standard rate for cabs. The cabbie jumped down, full of fight.

'What's this bleeding bob for?' he asked.

'Your fare, my man,' said Edward.

'A bleeding bob for two hours' driving and ten miles?' roared the cabbie. The lady of title quickly felt in her purse and gave him two sovereigns. 'That's better, mum,' he said, 'and thank'ee kindly. I knowd you was a lady as soon as I seen you—but where did you pick *'Im* up?'

It was a story which Edward often used to tell against himself.

On most occasions it was not thought necessary to hide situations or identities from either the husband of the lady concerned or the stable-staff of the Prince, and he used his own carriage. Victoria (Vita) Sackville-West, the writer whose lesbian love affair with Violet Trefusis has recently been made public, was a childhood friend of her inamorata when the girl was still Violet Keppel, Alice Keppel's daughter. She often used to call after lessons at the Keppels' house in Portman Square and see the King's conveyance waiting unostentatiously nearby—no painted four-in-hand with armorial bearings, but a discreet one-horse brougham with the groom sitting patiently on the box. And on occasion, as the butler received Vita in the hall, he would hustle her into a dark corner and mask her view as he explained, 'A gentleman is coming down.' And Majesty passed by.

Champagne diplomacy. King Edward, flanked by German warships seen through the windows of the Imperial Yacht Club at Kiel, remains unperturbed as he confronts Prince Henry of Prussia.

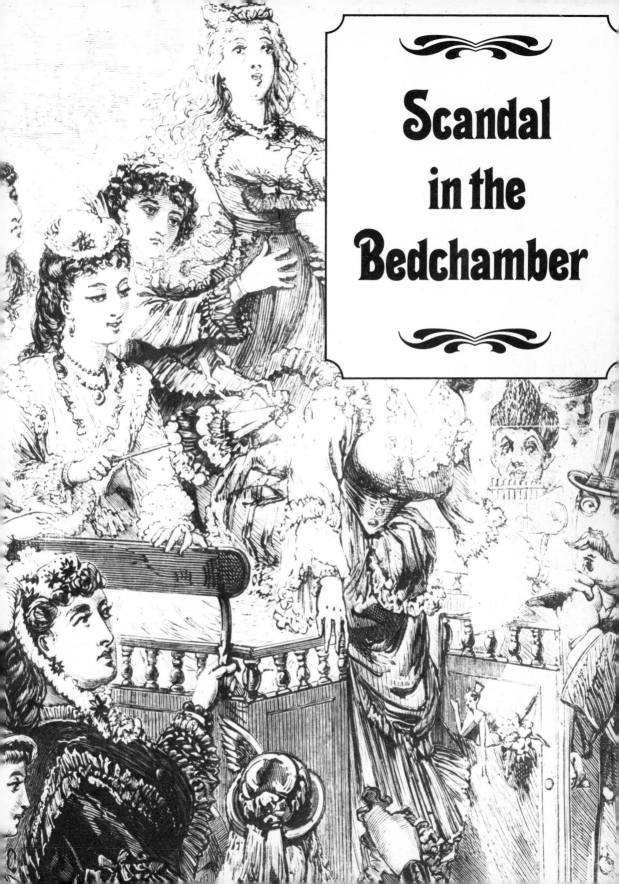

Scandal in the Bedchamber

IT was all boudoir-activity at this time of the day, and year of the century. Nevertheless, 'Scandal in the Bedchamber' is a key-phrase which is relevant to an understanding of much of Edward's sexual behaviour throughout his life. It was the psychological upset of such a scandal that hurried his mother, Queen Victoria, into the embrace of his father, Albert, at a time when she had decided not to marry him, at least for years, since she so much enjoyed being a new young queen with a very masculine, very doting prime minister. It was Albert's mature and diplomatic handling of another more political bedchamber crisis at Court which opened Victoria's eyes to the public potential of a consort whom she had originally, in Hanoverian despotism, intended to keep only for private pleasure. And that laid the foundation of an idolatrous veneration for him which finally did incalculable harm both to Victoria and to Edward.

It was Victoria's personal reaction to the intimacies of the bedchamber, particularly her revulsion against bearing the nine children Albert gave her, which governed much of her lifelong disgust at her first-born son 'with whom I suffered far the most severely.' And it was Albert's personal horror of *all* bedchamber scandal—especially as particularized for him by the libertinism of his father, the technical immorality of his wronged mother, the dissipation of his brother, and the debauchery of the long line of Victoria's 'wicked uncles', the seven wanton sons of King George III—that, allied with an abnormally male-orientated upbringing, ruled his attitude to *any* sexual adventures, but above all his son's. Son Edward understandably displayed an exaggerated reaction which was by no means a parallel revulsion. The prudery of the mid-Victorian age was not the consequence of Victoria but of Albert. Victoria, though she hated the aftermath of copulation, was a sensuous and passionate woman, whereas Albert was an unwilling capitulant to lust. 'Victorianism', in its derogatory sense, is very largely Albertianism.

Victoria and Albert were first cousins. Victoria's mother was the sister of Albert's father, the Duke of Saxe-Coburg-Gotha. Victoria was born as the result of a desperate effort by the third, fourth and seventh sons of the dying King George III to marry and produce an heir to the throne in due succession to the Prince Regent, later George IV. The third son was William, Duke of Clarence, aged fifty-three. The fourth son was Edward, Duke of Kent, aged fifty-one. William had discarded his mistress of twenty years' standing, the actress Mrs Dorothy Jordan, but did not disown their ten children. Edward put his mistress of twenty-seven years'

Edward, as Arbiter of Sport as well as Society, raced his yacht *Britannia, right,* in the intervals between giving parties aboard her. His son, later King George V, also pictured here, earnestly maintained the tradition.

standing, Madame de St Laurent, into a nunnery. William chose the German Princess Adelaide of Saxe-Meiningen. Edward chose the German Princess Victoria of Saxe-Coburg, later the Dowager Princess Charles of Leiningen, a widow of thirty-one with two surviving children.

The two brothers were married together at Kew on the same day, 13 July 1818. William's marriage produced a daughter who lived only seven hours. Two months after that birth and death, on 24 May 1819 at Kensington Palace, the Duchess of Kent was delivered of a healthy daughter by Madame Siebold, a rare woman with the university qualifications of physician and surgeon. After much bloody-mindedness over the baby's name, expressed at the font by the Prince Regent in front of the Archbishop of Canterbury who was christening her, the girl was baptized as Alexandrina Victoria, then regarded as Russian and German names, all the names with English connotations having been struck out on the spot by the crabbed Regent.

Five weeks later the obstetrician Madame Siebold brought into the world Victoria's cousin, Prince Albert of Saxe-Coburg-Gotha. It was planned from birth that the two cousins should marry eventually. Shortly afterwards, when Victoria was eight months old, her father, the Duke of Kent, died at Sidmouth, leaving his baby third in succession to the throne of Great Britain. Almost immediately, the death of old King George III made her second in line: her father and her grandfather were buried together. At the age of eleven, with her uncle William on the throne, she was Heiress Presumptive. At the age of eighteen she was queen.

She was plain, though with the passing glamour of youthfulness, petite—not five feet high—and with an embarrassing tendency to plumpness. After eighteen months as queen she was shocked to find she already weighed nine stones, and tried to cut out snacks and to stop drinking beer, which she liked. She had an instinctive rather than an inherent majesty; a beautiful speaking voice which was always described as 'silver'; and an appallingly hot temper. Above all she was gay. At her first State ball she danced till dawn, but not yet the waltz, since only Royalty was permitted to embrace her in the intimate manner of this measure. 'Royalty' then meant the direct family of a reigning sovereign, even if he was only the Sovereign Duke of Saxe-Coburg and Gotha. Victoria did once try the dance with the heir of the Czar of Russia, but it was left to Prince Albert of Saxe-Coburg-Gotha to teach it to her properly, after they were engaged. 'I did very well,' the Queen recorded, 'starting badly but finishing *brilliantly.'*

Overleaf. Legs, female, were forbidden spectacles outside the areas of theatrical dancing and after-supper relaxation, but suffered little competition from the shanks of the Gentlemen at Arms.

Left. Legs, male, suitably tight-trousered, attract an appreciative downward glance for Edward's son Prince Eddy, Duke of Clarence, who has since been nominated as a candidate for the identity of the untraced murderer Jack the Ripper.

Prince Albert was the second son of a sovereign. His father, Duke Ernest of Saxe-Coburg, married Luise, heiress of the Duke of Saxe-Gotha, and acquired the title to Gotha, making his whole dominion about half the size of an English county. After the birth of their two sons, Ernest and Albert, Duke Ernest abandoned his eighteen-year-old wife for a life of profligacy, and the Duchess eventually found her own consolation. She was consequently divorced, and married again, but died early of cancer when Albert was thirteen. Albert did not banish the image of his mother from his mind—one of his first gifts to Victoria was a brooch of hers. But neither did he become estranged from his father, whose reputation became increasingly blacker, nor from his brother, later Duke Ernest II, whose long and disreputable life gave him a body that was impotent and a personality that was actively shunned.

Ironically, it was not the pure Albert, but his sophisticated son Edward, moving as Prince of Wales in a constantly criticized circle of worldly and bohemian acquaintances, who was compelled to dart into the bushes when he saw Ernest approaching. On one visit to Paris, Edward was in the Bois de Boulogne when Duke Ernest drove past. 'There goes my uncle Ernest,' he said. 'When I see him

I look the other way, there are always some impossible women with him.'

Albert had an altogether different character from the males of his line. He was also, with his fair hair and blue eyes, of an entirely different colouring and physique. This led to false reports, very widely repeated, that he was illegitimate by a Jewish chamberlain of his mother's. At the age of seventeen, when she conceived Albert, the Duchess Luise had neither the inclination nor the opportunity for indiscretion, and the chamberlain was not even on the horizon at that time.

From the age of four Albert was brought up by men, and relied on them for emotional support as well as domestic service. This observation carries no sexual overtones, but Albert certainly grew up without an appreciation of women, a gap in his character which marriage and fatherhood only slowly and partially filled in.

Shortly before Albert presented himself for final inspection and appraisal by Victoria as her potential husband, he was sent to Italy on the normal cultural tour of a nineteen-year-old prince, which was also seen as an opportunity for him to sow his wild oats. He could not produce a single oat. This was not altogether a pleasant discovery for Victoria, who was then a worldly enough little minx in a very earthy court. But later she modified her reaction to one of relief, and finally to ineffable piety. Her definitive summing-up of the missed opportunities of that grand tour was, 'God knows, vice itself would ever have recoiled from the look alone of one who wore the lily of the blameless life.'

In spite of the ecstasy of this statement, which was made after Albert's death, there is no reason to doubt its message. Albert himself once volunteered in a private discussion the admission, 'I have never feared temptation with regard to women because I have no inclination in that respect, and that species of vice disgusts me.' He was being candid rather than priggish, for he did not always avoid discussion of sex, as a prude would. At least he tried to work out a moral attitude to it. 'Beloved Papa always said,' Victoria reported to her married daughter at a difficult time when Edward's younger brother Alfred (Duke of Edinburgh) was making passes at Edward's wife Alexandra only two months after their marriage, 'that feelings of admiration and even love are not sinful—nor can you prevent the impulses of one's nature, but it is your duty to avoid the temptation in every way.' It was a duty which Albert carried out very competently, even if it was realized that he had not passed this inclination on to his sons: The only way to rid Alfred of the temptation to compromise his brother's marriage was to send him away to sea, and when this was done he promptly got a lady into trouble in Malta. In spite of the arrangement made for them in their cradles, Albert's first visit to Victoria was made twelve months before she became queen, when they were both seventeen, and both aware that their eventual marriage was being urgently manoeuvred. Victoria reported to her matchmaking uncle, Leopold, King of the Belgians, 'how delighted I am with him, and how much I like him in every way. He possesses every quality that could be desired to make me perfectly happy.' A year later she was queen, absolutely unconcerned with marriage, completely taken up in a sort of intoxication with the glamour and success she was enjoying as a popular young sovereign. A crowded year passed, and in the midst of the gaiety surrounding her coronation she wrote to Leopold that Albert was in limbo and 'I am *very* anxious that it should be understood that I am *not* guilty of any breach of promise, for *I never gave any.'*

One year after that, Victoria was highly unpopular in the country, was hissed when she appeared in public, and declared that, if it were not for her coronation oath, she would abdicate and leave the country. Indications of Victoria's unpopularity were not confined to hissing. Aggressive vandalism reached even within the fortress of Windsor Castle. On the morning of 10 October 1839, stones were thrown through the windows of the Queen's dressing-room and three other rooms. In the evening of the same day Albert and his brother Ernest (who was now quietly nursing syphilis) arrived at Windsor at dinner-time and danced in the ballroom afterwards. Victoria sighed, almost swooning, 'Albert really is quite charming, and so excessively handsome, such beautiful blue eyes, an excellent nose, and such a pretty mouth with delicate mustachios and slight but very fine whiskers; a beautiful figure, broad in the shoulders and a fine waist. My heart is quite *going.'*

Next day her heart had quite gone, Within a week of Albert's arrival, Victoria proposed marriage to him. As if struck by a tornado, they collapsed into each others' arms. Victoria could not count the number of times they embraced. 'I am loved by such an Angel!' It was decided that they should be married within four months, and Victoria numbly hoped that somehow the state of marriage should reach perfection by not giving her any children. She had found her angel, but she saw no room in her life for cherubs.

The reason for Victoria's extraordinary swing from vigorous rejection of marriage to ecstatic acceptance of it was grounded in her whole-hearted and ill-judged protagonism in a Court scandal. Her own participation was excusable in a strong-willed but inexperienced girl not yet twenty. But it was totally unjustifiable on the part of the Prime Minister who abetted and encouraged her in the misjudgement—the sixty-year-old Lord Melbourne. There was existing scandal enough at Court. The Lord Chamberlain, the Marquess of Conyngham, had been a member of the Royal Household for seventeen years. For ten years of this period he had been deeply embarrassed by his mother. Lady Conyngham was the last and enduring mistress of King George IV, reigned as long as he did after the Regency, and prospered longer, annexing to herself that section of the National Anthem which suggests:

> Thy choicest gifts in store
> On her be pleased to pour.

Her perquisites included some of the Crown Jewels, which she graciously returned to the next king after George's death, and a further £100,000-worth of jewellery (the bills still exist) which she naturally did not resign.

But the King's inclination was not only towards Lady Conyngham. He cultivated the whole family, including Lord Conyngham, who witnessed, with what equanimity he could muster, the rouged monarch of sixty holding hands with Lady Conyngham under the table before indicating that it was bed-time. Their eldest son, the Earl of Mount Charles, left Court in disgust. His younger brother, Lord Francis Conyngham, stayed on, to be constantly hailed by the King as 'dearest Frank' and given the odd star and order. The Conyngham heir died, and dearest Frank became in succession Earl of Mount Charles and Marquess of Conyngham, and a great courtier in his own right. Under King William IV he was installed as Lord Chamberlain, the highest office at Court, offering both personal and political prestige.

When he retained this office after Victoria's accession, he had shaken off the memory of his earlier mortification sufficiently to introduce his own mistress into the Household and give her the position of Palace Housekeeper, although his own wife was still at Court. Occasionally the Chamberlain and the Housekeeper could be spotted, like love-birds, swooping into each other's embrace after absences of an hour or more. The Conynghams were clearly a demonstrative if not an uxorious family.

Conyngham in his turn extended his indulgence. The officer of the Household next in precedence to himself was the Lord Steward. This position was held by the Earl of Uxbridge, a relative of

Conyngham's wife, and Uxbridge was permitted to instal his own mistress into a Court appointment.

These unconventional arrangements were perfectly well known to the young Queen Victoria, who accepted the situation as part of her royal legacy, and who indeed strongly patronized the family which most obviously perpetuated this permissive regime, the Pagets, led by Lord Uxbridge and the second Lady Conyngham. Victoria was also well aware that her Prime Minister, Lord Melbourne, had had extreme difficulty in extricating himself after being cited in two divorce actions, an escape from disgrace of which it was said at the time 'no man's luck can go further.' Far from recoiling from Lord Melbourne, Victoria was attracted to him. The courtier Charles Greville, who was Clerk to the Privy Council, declared that Victoria's inclination towards Melbourne was 'sexual, but she does not know it', and that Melbourne was 'passionately fond of her . . . because he is a man with a capacity for loving without having anything in the world to love.' Victoria later revealed that Albert had convinced her that, in her fascination for Melbourne, 'I worked myself up to what really became quite foolish.'

In view of the murky climate at Court, which was later cleared when Albert took over substantial domestic control, it would seem improbable that Victoria and Melbourne together could bring the Court into further and unnecessary disrepute. Yet this is what occurred through their behaviour over the unpleasant affair of Lady Flora Hastings and Sir John Conroy.

Lady Flora was, in 1839, an intelligent but somewhat waspish female of thirty-three, looking something like Miss Rachael Wardle in *The Pickwick Papers* (which had recently been published). Five years earlier, she had been wished on Victoria as a lady-in-waiting by Victoria's mother, the Duchess of Kent. Victoria found her antipathetic, and after the accession she was confined to the household of the Duchess of Kent. But the Duchess was firmly installed in Buckingham Palace until she was removed on Victoria's marriage, and this situation gave Lady Flora residence at Court and limited access to the Queen.

Sir John Conroy was the saturnine Comptroller of the Household to the Duchess of Kent, a position which certainly enabled him to embezzle £60,000, and reputedly led him to the bed of the Duchess as her lover. Melbourne himself believed this scandal, but there is now no proof whatsoever. Victoria, with her extreme passions, hated Conroy extravagantly. 'He is capable of every villainy,' was her belief.

Sir John Conroy certainly embezzled the money for Victoria's upkeep, less certainly climbed into her mother's bed.

In the winter of 1838, Sir John Conroy shared with Lady Flora Hastings a long coach-trip from Edinburgh to London, including an overnight journey. In January 1839, Queen Victoria, observing the figure of Lady Flora, decided that she was pregnant. She consulted Melbourne, who jauntily said that it might be so, but time would tell, and nothing should be done about it. Unfortunately, Victoria decided to do something about it, fired by her dislike of Lady Flora and her hatred for Sir John Conroy. 'She is with child', she wrote in her journal. 'The horrid cause of all this is the Monster and Demon Incarnate, whose name I forbear to mention, but which is the first word of the second line on this page.'

Toe-warming, coffee, gossip and picture-albums as the unliberated Victorian ladies await the gentlemen after dinner. Edward, in his maturity, was to cut the duration of this sexless interval.

Reference to the journal shows that the code is deciphered by the initials 'J.C.' which stand for John Conroy.

In a court full of gossiping Ladies of the Bedchamber, Victoria had ample opportunity to sanction savage reprisals, if only by belatedly following Melbourne's advice to do nothing. Unavoidably it became public knowledge in Society that the Queen was not neutral in the Palace vendetta. The women at Court forced a humiliating medical examination on Lady Flora. She was declared a virgin, though with an abnormal enlargement of the belly. Melbourne unnecessarily mentioned to the Queen that even certified virgins could sometimes be pregnant. Queen Victoria, however, virtually apologized to Lady Flora, and then, under the pressure of events, speedily recanted her compassion.

Sir John Conroy, for his part, backed by the Duchess of Kent, urged Lady Flora to get her relatives to expose the Queen's indiscreet partiality. The controversy became fully public. In the middle of it, Melbourne's Whig Government toppled, and extremists among the incoming Tories openly threatened that they would expel the majority of Victoria's Ladies of the Bedchamber, who were considered to have fomented the gossip, and who were in any case the wives of Whig magnates. Sir Robert Peel, the Tory leader, was summoned to the Palace and indicated that he would desire the replacement of *some* of the most political Ladies. Victoria unjustifiably distorted this attitude, in a letter to Melbourne which she speedily convinced herself was absolute truth, saying that Peel 'has insisted on my giving up my Ladies, to which I replied that I never would consent, and I never saw a man so frightened. . . . This is infamous. . . . Keep yourself in readiness, for you may soon be wanted.'

As played by Victoria, this move was backstairs political intrigue of a most accomplished sophistication. And she forced Sir Robert Peel to accept that he had presented the 'Bedchamber Question' as a threat to all her Ladies (which he had never intended) and as the touchstone deciding her approval of him as Prime Minister. She manoeuvred Peel into declining office because he had not her confidence over the Bedchamber Crisis, and she sent again for Melbourne, and kept him in power for two more years in a situation of see-saw parliamentary majorities. 'What a blessed and unexpected escape!' wrote this capable girl of nineteen.

Politically, this defiance and rejection of a constitutionally sound alternative Government made Victoria unpopular as a queen regnant. But the rolling swell of political unpopularity had already been capped by the breakers of social derision whipped up by the public airing of the case of Lady Flora. Carefully fed by the

Sir Robert Peel was skilfully out-manoeuvred by Queen Victoria over the 'Bedchamber Question'.

Sir James Clark, Queen Victoria's doctor, who had declared Lady Flora Hastings pregnant, was later compelled to write a certificate testifying that she was undoubtedly a virgin. 'Anyone can make a mistake or two,' said the airy physician.

understandably partisan and temperamentally choleric Hastings family, with timely prods of the poker from Sir John Conroy, the London Press blazed with the details of the scandal, and scorched both Queen and Prime Minister with their insults. Victoria said she could have hanged the editor of the *Morning Post* and the whole Hastings family for their 'infamy'. Domestically, Melbourne only worsened the situation by undignified sympathetic bitchiness which intensified Victoria's increasingly irrational feelings against Lady Flora and, by contagion, against her own mother, the Duchess of Kent. In her confusion, the Queen discussed with Lord Melbourne the possibility of her marriage as a means of escaping from the aura of her mother and her mother's household. As soon as she put the proposition into words, she shied from its implications, saying that there was no need to marry for three or four years.

Lady Flora Hastings grew worse in health, while her appearance of pregnancy increased. Within two months of Victoria's triumph over Sir Robert Peel, she died in Buckingham Palace. A post mortem showed a gross tumour on the liver. Her death reinvigorated the public outcry against the personal part which the Queen had taken in her disgrace. When the Loyal Toast was given at public dinners it was received in silence. Whenever Victoria appeared in public, too often riding in Rotten Row with Lord Melbourne, she was hooted. 'I would have them flogged!' roared the young Queen when she learned the identity of two peeresses who had hissed her at Ascot. In anguish and depression, the Queen actually lost a little weight.

She revived a little at the prospect of family gaiety with the visits of young men from among her kinsfolk in Russia and Germany. In the autumn Cousin Albert arrived, and Victoria was in love. She furiously reviled herself for her decision to keep him waiting for three or four years 'at the risk of ruining all his prospects in life.' They were married, not amid universal acclamation. The Opposition defeated the Government and reduced the State income voted to Albert to little more than half. And still a satirist wrote:

> He comes to take, 'for better or for worse',
> England's fat Queen, and England's fatter purse.

At the next change of Government it was Prince Albert who sent his secretary secretly to Sir Robert Peel proposing a slight change in the personnel of the Ladies of the Bedchamber. This was accepted. There was never another Bedchamber Crisis.

By this time the Queen was pregnant with the future Prince of Wales. The one thing which Victoria dreaded about marriage had happened. She had, she said, 'the greatest horror of having children. . . . I would rather have none.' And the ultra-observant Charles Greville, prowling round Windsor Castle at 8.30 in the morning (long before the Queen was usually up) after the Queen's wedding night, and seeing the couple out walking, muttered, 'This is not the way to provide us with a Prince of Wales.' Nevertheless, 285 days later Victoria gave birth to a daughter, and ten weeks after that was infuriated to find that she was pregnant again.

Five born and four to come. Winterhalter's famous portrait of Victoria and Albert with Vicky, 6, Edward, 4, Alice, 3, Alfred, 2, and the newly-born Helena.

It was a state she deeply resented, believing that pregnancy ruined her relationship with her husband, and childbirth made a woman 'like a dog or a cow'. There was a touch of the spirit of women's liberation in her attitude. She saw a woman's 'submission' to sex as 'with one small act to abdicate all her rights to another, and to a man!' She declared that 'those very selfish men would not bear for a minute what we poor slaves have to endure.' Later she developed such a fixation that she even censored the Marriage Service of her daughters, 'purifying it of its worst coarsenesses' by omitting from the Church's ancient recital the first two reasons for matrimony: that it was ordained for the procreation of children, and for a remedy against sin and to avoid fornication. All that was left for her children officially to hope for was 'the mutual society, help, and comfort, that the one ought to have of the other.' And this was enough to make Victoria weep fresh tears, for by this time she had lost Albert.

On 9 November 1841, Queen Victoria gave birth to a 'fine large Boy'. He caused her more pain than any other of her children, and in a rare moment of candid introspection she once declared that in his boyhood she caused him more pain, in retribution. What she never admitted, and what was far more important, was that she persecuted him by wilful neglect much more effectively *after* his boyhood. The reason for this was that his first youthful folly occurred relatively near to his father's death, and she falsely connected the two. She then extended the 'punishment' to deprive him of any effectively statesmanlike career for forty years. It was a disproportionate penance to exact for one slip, and it was badly judged because it gave time and opportunity for many more. Shaw once categorized our 'two tyrannous physical passions: concupiscence and chastity. We become mad in pursuit of sex; we become equally mad in the persecution of that pursuit.' Neither the Widow of Windsor nor her worldly son were really basically concerned with the flagellation or the cultivation of lust. Yet they give the impression of having pursued these objectives, though perhaps in the same manner that was attributed to the exploiters and expanders of the British Empire, 'almost in a fit of absence of mind'. Victoria and Edward were incompatible by temperament but antagonistic only by accident. It was in their nature that they would shape different courses in life. But they scattered at the first storm, and set off for unnecessarily distant destinations. Their mutual shame was not in having once been foolish, but in not discontinuing their folly.

The 'fine large Boy' who was to develop into the 48-inch-girth Man.

'Young America'

HE first tutor assigned to the Prince of Wales had the ominous name of Birch, and he by no means disdained corporal punishment. He had been captain of the school at Eton under the headmastership of 'Flogger' Keate, whose record was ninety strokes of the birch at one exposure.

Edward was kept away from Eton, and from any school, not because of the flogging-block but because of the playing fields. His father Albert did not consider organized games, still less the adventure of games individually invented by schoolboy buccaneers, conducive to learning. When Edward was aged ten, and Birch and a team of tutors had worked on him for three years, Birch was able to report to the royal parents that appropriate *severe punishment* had begun to work on the boy's extreme disobedience and unwillingness to submit to discipline, but there were still too many instances of unshakable sullen silence and apparent mental disintegration, though the boy 'always evinced a most forgiving disposition after I had punished him.'

The lad was, in fact, under Albert's instructions, worked far too hard, until in desperation he resorted to ungovernable fits of temper, bouts of rage which in an adult would be considered manic, or spells of complete mental collapse. Edward's head tutor was told by Baron Stockmar, *éminence grise* behind Victoria and Albert, that the boy *was* exhibiting signs of madness: first as 'an exaggerated copy of his mother' (whom Stockmar had already accused of madness during her frenzied management of the Bedchamber Plot), second as an inheritance from the allegedly mad King George III. In truth, all Victoria's older children were ruthlessly overworked and overdisciplined, and they all responded with the same irrational fury. The Princess Royal (Vicky), the Prince of Wales, and Princess Alice, the three of them born within thirty months, all displayed the same symptoms of violent temper in youth, often expressing their frustration by beating their heads against the floor or the wall until they were speechless, although they were of varied intelligence.

Victoria occasionally complained in confidence about her husband's harshness, which seems to have grown from an exaggerated fixation on the debaucheries of Victoria's 'wicked uncles'. Before Edward was two years old, Albert told Lord Wriothesley that the 'greatest object must be to make the boy as unlike as possible to any of his great-uncles', though Wriothesley thought Albert's father 'by far the worst of the family'. Albert, on the other hand, regretted far more explicitly to Lord Clarendon the severity of the Queen towards Edward, which he, Albert, had not sufficiently resisted because he feared the effect on her mind when she was crossed in

Edward with his brother Alfred, later Duke of Edinburgh, and their tutor Frederick Gibbs, who deliberately exhausted the boys daily, and when they were prostrated declared that the madness of their ancestor George III was repeating itself.

a rage, and which had led to the 'aggressive treatment of the Prince of Wales' which was 'perhaps a mistake' (for Albert, as well as Birch, had been called on to whip the boy). Albert said that the 'disagreeable office of punishment had always fallen upon him, and he hesitated to resist the harshness of the Queen.'

There were many witnesses at Court to what Palmerston called the Queen's 'unconquerable aversion' to the Prince of Wales. When the boy was only six, Charles Greville, commenting that the Queen called her son 'stupid', suggested that 'the hereditary and unfailing antipathy of our Sovereigns to their Heirs Apparent seems this early to be taking root.'

Victoria certainly referred sarcastically, not only to her son's alleged stupidity, but to his ugliness. In over forty references to Edward contained in her edited letters to her eldest daughter between 1858 and 1861 there is only one approving remark. Otherwise he is castigated for his 'systematic idleness', 'stupidity', 'dullness', 'mediocrity', but above all for his appearance. When he wears Court dress with knee-breeches, he is called 'Knock-kneed'. At other times he is chinless and 'not at all in good looks'. Albert's paternal and Victoria's maternal grandmother had had a very large nose which she passed on to many of her descendants; Victoria detested this nose, particularly when she saw it sprouting on Edward. 'The nose is becoming the true Coburg nose', she wailed when he was eighteen, 'and begins to hang a little, but there remains unfortunately the want of chin, which with that large nose and very large lips is not so well in profile.' Still harping on the same theme, she notes that 'his nose and mouth are too enormous, and as he pastes his hair down to his head and wears his clothes frightfully—he really is anything but good looking. That coiffure

A prophetic picture of Edward in the guise of Bacchus, aged twelve.

Accustomed early to the kilt by his German father, Edward wore Highland costume well in spite of his mother's allegation that he had knock knees. His bag in this portrait is small. In 1890, in a ten-day shoot organised for Edward in Hungary by Baron Hirsch, ten guns killed 20,000 grouse.

is really too hideous with his small head and enormous features.'

Doubtless many a mother has regarded her teen-age son with similar distress, but few have been so outspoken in their dislike. Victoria seems early to have written off the Prince of Wales as a suitable successor to her throne: 'The greatest improvement, I fear, will never make him fit for his position. His only safety, and the country's, is in his implicit reliance, in everything, on Dearest Papa, that perfection of human beings!'

It was a disastrous way to bring up a future king, and Bertie, the name he was finally given in the family after some years of being called, distastefully, 'the Boy', inevitably reacted.

In spite of his mother's disapproval of his looks, many strangers found him attractive and even handsome. At the age of fourteen he captured the hearts of the French when, with his sister, he accompanied his parents on a first State visit to Paris, to the Court of the Emperor Napoleon III and the beautiful Empress Eugénie. For much of the time Edward wore the kilt, to great popular acclaim in spite of his supposed knock-knees. The French royal couple greatly endeared themselves to the Prince of Wales, who begged the Empress to ask Victoria to allow the children to stay longer at the French Court. The Empress tactfully countered that his parents, returning to England, would not be able to do without the children there. 'Not do without us!' said Edward impulsively. 'Don't fancy that! There are six more of us at home, and they don't want us!'

The Boy was growing in perception, and in aspiration, though he was never trained to discipline his desires. Normally he displayed quite extraordinarily considerate manners, but, since he had never been schooled to rough.it with companions who gave him no precedence, he was always inclined to assume that he could have what he wanted in a social context: and he grabbed it. When he was sixteen he went on a reading party to Germany, with four Eton boys of his age and four tutors. On the first night he took a glass of wine too many, saw a pretty girl, kissed her, and got his face slapped. He soon learned how to take his liquor, though not so soon how to take his women. A few months later, Queen Victoria recorded that 'Bertie had a sick head-ache yesterday, from imprudence', and that is virtually the last reference ever made to Edward as unable to take his tipple. He was, in fact, when he became a leader of Society, an outstanding influence in making alcoholic temperance (not teetotalism) fashionable. Where gentlemen once used to down two bottles of claret when the ladies had left the dinner-table, they followed the Prince of Wales in taking only a glass of brandy with their coffee. The Prince's purpose was not idealistic: he was in a hurry to rejoin the ladies.

On his seventeenth birthday the young Prince of Wales began briefly to be steered towards independence. His tutors were dismissed and he was given a Grenadier Colonel, Robert Bruce, as governor. But he was told by his parents that he could not hide behind this governor from the consequences of any of his actions, but would have to bear the responsibility himself. This homily was largely wind from Albert's abundant flatulence, for Colonel Bruce, as might be expected, 'governed' Edward pretty effectively. The Prince was also given younger equerries who served in rotation, two of them being army officers who had won the Victoria Cross at the age of twenty-four in the recent Crimean War.

In an extraordinary briefing document to these equerries, Prince Albert listed his priorities with a pompous introduction on 'Appearance, Deportment and Dress':

A gentleman does not indulge in careless self-indulgent ways, such as lolling in armchairs or on sofas, slouching in his gait, or placing himself in unbecoming attitudes with his hands in his pockets. He will borrow nothing from the fashions of the groom or the game-keeper, and whilst avoiding the frivolity and foolish vanity of dandyism, will take care that his clothes are of the best quality.

This is a muted example of the extraordinary preoccupation with dress, insignia, and the minutiae of uniform which is still characteristic of the British Royal Family after a century and a half. When Victoria came to the throne and visited King William IV's mourning widow at Windsor, she gave explicit instructions as to whether a flag flying at half-mast should or should not be raised when she entered the Castle. Prime Minister Melbourne, who received these instructions, said nonchalantly that he had 'never thought of the flag, or knew anything about it'. King Edward, with his fifty military uniforms and his extreme sensitivity about the wearing of Orders by his courtiers, was in general a martinet on protocol, but once, in what he thought was an extremity of tact, went to comic lengths to make his reproof friendly. His intimate friend and comrade in lady-killing, the Marquis de Soveral, Portuguese Ambassador, was a guest at Sandringham for a house-party for members of the Greek Royal Family. Edward knew that de Soveral had been given a Greek Order and, noticing that he was not wearing it at table, thought the Greeks would be offended. Having already flashed his own Greek Order, he cautiously unpinned it, groped under the table-cloth, and precariously fixed it to the bottom of Soveral's waistcoat.

Queen Victoria, though insistent to Edward in his youth that he should not wear new-fashioned clothes that were 'extravagant' or 'slang'—'because it would be an offence against decency, leading to an indifference to what is morally wrong'—almost immediately complained that Bertie 'showed not a particle of attention to anything but dress!' 'Even when out shooting he is more occupied with his trousers than with the game!'

For his seventeenth birthday his parents created Edward a knight of the Garter, which demanded elaborate dressing-up, and gave him the uniform and cocked hat of a lieutenant-colonel, 'which he was as eager about as Arthur [aged eight] would have been at a [toy] bearskin and sword'. Yet Edward's own private complaint was that he hated receiving the uniform because he wanted to start a proper army career, as a subaltern and not as a colonel.

With Colonel Bruce and his young equerry, Edward wore his new uniform on a visit to Berlin, and left it behind on a trip to Rome which he took immediately afterwards, travelling incognito as Baron Renfrew. He stayed for three months on what was meant to be a cultural visit. But, although he met Robert Browning, he showed more enthusiasm for the theatre, which at that time was a lively art in Italy. He attended the first performance of *Un Ballo in Maschera* and met its composer, Verdi. Masks, which had been banned in Rome for ten years, were permitted at the great Carnival festivities that year, and Edward was given a balcony on the Corso from which he threw flowers, confetti and gifts to 'the beautiful charmeuses who passed slowly along in their carriages'. Colonel Bruce had forbidden him to participate in the last great night of merriment, but the Prince doggedly telegraphed to his mother and, surprisingly, was given permission to celebrate. In an audience with Pius IX he made the not unperceptive remark to the Pope, 'Your Holiness reigns over a magnificent city which can pass from the unrestrained and innocent amusement of the Mardi Gras to the penitence of Ash Wednesday. But we, the men of the North, cannot interrupt our pleasures so rapidly.' But Edward did cool down, and there is some characteristic dignity in the phrase with which the youth declined to attend the Holy Week services at St Peter's. 'At Rome', he said, 'a Protestant especially should show his attachment to his own church.'

From Rome Edward went to Edinburgh, to begin cramming for a spell of four terms' residence at Oxford University. He interrupted his time at Oxford with an extended trip, in the Long Vacation, to North America.

The visit to Canada and the United States in 1860 was sheer personal triumph all the way. It was the earliest exercise of the new British Empire in the technique of the public-relations power of royalty, and the young man of eighteen performed magnificently. Unfortunately, it was the last time for forty years that Edward was entrusted with these responsibilities. An unimportant folly, coinciding with the death of his father, hardened his mother's heart against encouraging him to follow his true métier. Never again, until he was king, was he able to register such full diplomatic achievement through the influence of his warm personality.

The Prince set out from Plymouth in mid-July in the prestige steam-screw/sailing warship *Hero* (91 guns). In his suite was the portly and pompous Duke of Newcastle, who, as the ineffective head of a creaking army machine, had resigned as Secretary for War in the middle of the Crimean campaign but was now back in politics as Secretary of State for the Colonies. The suite also included the Lord Steward of the Queen's Household, the Prince's governor and equerries, and the Regius Professor of Medicine at Oxford who travelled as the Prince's physician. The *Saturday*

Edward proudly wears his Colonel's uniform at the age of 17.

With Edward aboard, HMS *Hero* sails from Plymouth for the triumphal tour of North America.

Review sped the parting guest with the condescending advice which leader-writers spew only too easily: 'Will not the coolness of his youthful head be rather severely tried by the incense of loyalty—that incense whose overpowering fumes give Kings only too much right to be destitute of common sense?' But the journal did go on to make a comment which was ironically true of the later career of the Prince, in his years of enforced idleness in spite of his success on the American tour. 'Public action,' it reminded the Queen, 'is probably the best antidote to those corrupting and degrading influences which beset the youth of Princes. It is indolence, joined to passion and opportunity, that has too often made the history of an heir apparent one of family misery and personal disgrace.'

A fortnight later the *Hero* and her attendant frigate the *Ariadne*, then the fastest warships in the world, reached St John's, Newfoundland. It was not the most glamorous spot to begin a royal tour, and the torrential rain forced the Prince to delay his disembarkation for some hours: heavy rain washed out or forced the postponement of many civic welcomes during the tour, doused firework displays but never dampened the feverish enthusiasm of the spectators who came out by the ten thousands. Eventually the first of the many elaborate ceremonies of a royal landing was carried out, with the enormous yards of the *Hero* manned by standing sailors and the thud and smoke of the royal salute from the battleship's cannon setting the seagulls wheeling. Ashore, behind the nervous reader of the loyal address, there were the squares and files of the welcoming organizations who were to become familiar for their long and domewhat ill-drilled processions of entry: the Masonic Body, St Andrews's Society, St George's Society, the British Mechanics' Society (an embryo trade union), the Coopers' Society, the Temperance Society, the Native Society, the Irish Society, the Phoenix Voluntary Fire Company, and a guard of honour from the Royal Newfoundland Corps and four battalions of the Volunteers' Rifle Corps.

As was to be the pattern throughout the tour, there was a grand evening ball. Though London newspaper correspondents were assiduous enough, the North American tour was notable for the keen interest it evoked in the United States through the descent of a massive contingent from the New York press corps. Their comments were objective, salty, and entirely beneficial. Of that first ball, the *New York Herald* noted: 'The dancing, on the whole, among the company, was not very good. The Prince very affably and good-naturedly corrected some of the blundering dancers, and every now and then called out the different figures of the dance.' Energetically, he did not give up till three in the morning, justified his reputation as a graceful dancer, went aboard and sailed away.

The next stop was at Halifax, Nova Scotia, which had been converted into a 'perfect bower of greenery' by the erection of arches of triumph, sometimes thirty to a street, all decorated with flags and evergreen. Here the Royal Navy gave a ball aboard another 91-gun battleship, the *Nile*. The upper deck and poop were covered with drapery and bunting, and decorated with garlands of flowers. The guns had been slung below (they were still the old Nelsonian roller-mountings) and in every emplacement there was a mirror, with pictures painted on linen in every port-hole. At the ball ashore, the Prince opened the festivities by dancing a quadrille with the wife of the Lieutenant-Governor and a waltz with the Prime Minister's niece. 'After this he chose his partners without any special reference to their station. He converses fluently while dancing, and so freely as sometimes to interrupt the order of the dance.'

At Halifax, too, Victorian commercialism began its take-over:

Even in advertisements, the Prince's name or title is mysteriously connected with the Halifax national dish of pork and beans, or used as a puff for mild cider. You can't sit down to dinner but his portrait looms dimly from beneath the gravy in the centre of the plate. It is

Edward is greeted in triumph in Halifax.

Prince's hats, Prince's boots, Prince's coats, Prince's umbrellas; the whole land nods, in fact, with Prince's coronets and feathers.

The fleet sailed west to the Atlantic shore of New Brunswick before curving back into the Gulf of St Lawrence. Going up the St John river to Fredericton in a pinnace, the Prince directed that cheers from the banks should be answered by the ship's steam whistle and the Marine band. Many of the places visited were then provincial even by Canadian standards, and were not spared criticism by the New York pressmen, who at that time used the term 'slow' for country hickdom. At Charlottetown, Prince Edward Island, the *New York Times* special correspondent reported:

The people, having worn out their lungs and acquired headaches of the most distressful character from drinking bad liquors, have a woebegone appearance.

There was a levée this morning at which, of course, dress was imperative. And, white cravats being an article not cultivated in this *slow* place, many old gentlemen tied things exactly like table-cloths and towels round their necks. It was amusing to watch the twinkle in the Prince's eye as some of these men shuffled past him.

There was a review of the volunteers after the levée, which I did not go to see, for many of the militiamen were so brutally drunk last night that I could not hope for steadiness in the ranks today.

Quebec, as Edward saw it in 1860.

Three weeks passed before the great cannonade of the royal salute echoed off the high cliff of Quebec Castle, and it was pouring with rain again. The New York press contingent, who had had time to prospect, reported very favourably on the appearance of the women:

I have been particularly struck with and pleased by the Canadian ladies. Their dress is very peculiar, neat and becoming. A little hat of straw, formed like that of a man's, with no rim save a turned-up edge; a net which, hanging down upon the shoulders, contains the hair; a neat stuff-cloak and pretty little kid-boots complete the costume, the effect of which is charmingly heightened by the long feathers or plumes which gracefully swing off from the band of the hat. The effect is that all the girls look rather handsome and slightly coquettish.

As for the Prince, perhaps for the first time, he was submitted to an objective public appraisal:

I like him. He seems to be about five feet four inches high, his eye is beautifully blue, mild, funny, clear and jolly. His nose is well-defined, not perfectly straight, but clean-cut and prominent. His mouth is full and rather sensual, and his chin retreats wonderfully. His countenance indicates a happy-dispositioned, good-natured, humorous fun-loving boy, who knows what he is after and can't easily be fooled. He was dressed in the full uniform of a Colonel in the Royal Army, wearing a cocked hat, red coat with red and blue bands, black pants, patent leather boots and spurs, and very ill-fitting, soiled white gloves.

As the Prince came ashore there was a considerable amount of shuffling, manoeuvring and muttered comment among the official party, since great feeling had been aroused among the French and Irish residents of Quebec concerning the priority of position held, or captured, by the Roman Catholic and the Anglican bishop. An elaborate procession was then begun, 'during which an immense bouquet fell into the Prince's lap, whereupon he took off his chapeau, rose and bowed with a comical look at a very fair damsel, who blushingly returned his salute'.

But the *entrée d'honneur* was not, in the eyes of sophisticated observers, an entire success. Howard of the *New York Times* wrote:

I regret to say that the 'Triumphal Procession' was a humbug, a failure, and a complete non-success. The societies staggered along the line, with a portion of their members in uniform and a larger number without it. Some of them carried unmbrellas under their arms, and others over their heads, some of them wore hats, some caps, some marched four abreast and others marched or strammed along in single file.
Then there would be a long gap in the procession, after which half a score of chaps with banners or instruments of musical torture would

walk listlessly by and annoy every American who witnessed their intolerable *slowness* beyond all description.

On the day after his arrival the Prince attended church:

> The party occupied a box in the gallery and remained during the entire service.[1] The Prince wore a large black silk hat which was not becoming, a black frock-coat and pants with a white vest. During the service he did as everyone else did, looked all round the church, looked at the Bishop, at the girls, at the crowds, and at the ceiling, and after service was over, walked quietly to his carriage and jumped lightly from the ground to his seat, which being a distance of about four feet, was a very fair gymnastic performance considering it was Sunday, and that some two thousand people were looking at him as closely as ever a mouse was watched by a kitten.

Among the attendants at the church, apart from the devout and the voyeur, was a squad of New York pickpockets who realized the social importance of the occasion.

One took £420 from a gentleman's pocket, and another stole £50 from the Speaker of the House. A further tally of money and watches made an additional toll of £600 stolen from the congregation. The pickpockets were operating in the streets and public places, and then moved into the hotels, to the disgust of the press corps. 'In the best hotel in this city,' reported a London *Times* man with indignation, 'some gentlemen's bedrooms were skilfully opened and a clean sweep made of all money and watches. The artist of the *Illustrated London News* lost a considerable amount of property, and the correspondent of the *New York Tribune* was mulcted of a watch and chain worth £31.'

But there were other light-fingered gentry, or gentlewomen—the souvenir hunters. While the Prince was ashore (he was staying with the Governor-General, Sir Edmund Head) a party of ladies was invited aboard HMS *Hero*. They darted down to the cabin occupied by the Prince of Wales and 'stole every pin, every piece of wax, and all the knick-knacks that they could find there, as souvenirs of his Royal Highness. . . . One damsel was caught trying on his overcoat, from which every button had been cut by devotees of the youthful Guelph.' It was a fact that one enterprising (and ingenious) admirer, coming across his wash-basin, tipped the water out into a container provided by a bribed sailor, and sold the dirty water afterwards at four shillings a phial.

---

1 Perhaps a comment on the occupation of a box at the opera, where the nobs often arrived only for the second act and left before the last.

The Prince had to undertake a considerable amount of public speaking. When loyal addresses were delivered to him in the principal cities, it was generally his lot to read back an expression of appreciation. One American described his diction as 'sweet and low. He possesses one of the clearest, fullest and best modulated voices I ever heard, and its *sympathetic* tones excite a magnetic influence upon the hearer.' Another reported: 'The Queen is noted for the extreme particularity which she gives the full sound of the letter 'R' while the Prince never pronounces it distinctly.' This was fair transatlantic perception. At home, where accents were much more keenly analysed, Edward was mocked through all his life for his 'German accent', particularly for the 'burr' which he gave to his R's. It was a peculiarity which he must have caught from his father, since Victoria, although her first language was German, spoke very pure English.

In Lower Canada the loyal addresses were delivered and answered in French and English, and Howard of the *New York Times* reported that the Prince read his responses 'in both languages clearly, distinctly and sweetly'.

Nonetheless problems arose. When the Prince acknowledged a loyal address and an honorary degree from the University of Laval, he referred to the Roman Catholic bishops there as 'Gentlemen' although there had been a specific request that they should be acknowledged as 'My Lords'. In reply to an inevitable protest, the Duke of Newcastle framed his explanation so smoothly that, in turn, he offended the powerful extreme Protestants of the Orange Order in Upper Canada whom the whole operation had been intended to conciliate. In retaliation, the Orangemen, working through their Masonic lodges, instigated the serious riots which were considered the only blot on the tour.

After a highly successful visit to Montreal, Edward laid the foundation stone of a new Federal Parliament building at Ottawa, and steamed up the St Lawrence to confront the angry Orangemen, who had the political objective of compelling him as representative of the Crown, to do public homage to their own narrow-minded travesty of the principles of the Protestant Revolution of 1689-90, and of getting him to mouth the slogans attributed to their puppet, King Billy (William of Orange).

The Duke of Newcastle, an alert if over-rigid politician, was determined that this manoeuvre should not take place. With admirable generalship, Newcastle chose as his battleground the first possible confrontation. This was at the scheduled next stop of the tour, Kingston, Ontario, which the Prince was fast approaching by

The end crowns the work: completion of the Victoria Bridge over the St Lawrence river at Montreal, 1860.

Impressive craftsmanship from the silversmiths responsible for this trowel with which Edward sealed the completion of the Victoria Bridge in Montreal on his Canadian tour.

steamer. With even more speed the Orangemen of Ontario were erecting Orange arches over every road the Prince could possibly take. These were arches based on that at Londonderry, bristling with Orange banners, portraits of King Billy, and near-obscene anti-Papist slogans. In addition the Orangemen were drumming up all their forces for marches and demonstrations on the Prince's arrival.

Newcastle wrote in advance to the Mayor of Kingston requesting that there should be no anti-Catholic demonstration when the Prince came. The Corporation decided that, in spite of this request, the arches should remain and the processions be held. When the Prince's steamer arrived, a demonstration of 2000 militant Orangemen was waiting. Newcastle went ashore and warned the Mayor that the Prince would not land unless the waiting marchers were dispersed and the arches taken down. The Mayor asked for an overnight adjournment so that a decision could be taken in a cooler atmosphere. He called a joint meeting of the Corporation and the heads of the local Masonic lodge. Fortified by large supplies of liquor, the conference produced the opposite of a *détente*. It was decided that the Prince of Wales must be taught a lesson about Upper Canada. Long after midnight a motion was proposed and carried that 'the Prince should be invited either to land and be decorated with the Orange colours, or go to Hell and take his flunkeys with him.' The loyal address which the Mayor had already promised Newcastle would only be presented if the Prince came ashore and took part in an Orange procession.

The Prince's steamer immediately sailed away, hissed and booed and cursed from the shore. The next stop was to be Belleville. Even the Orangemen of Belleville were shocked by the violence at Hamilton, and they voted that they should take down their arches and cancel all processions. But a strong Orange contingent marched from Hamilton and prevented this from happening. The Prince's steamer moored at Belleville. Newcastle went ashore again to negotiate. He declined the counsel of a local Member of Parliament who advised that the party should come ashore and shut their eyes, when they would hear 30,000 people shouting with loyalty against 2000 disaffected bigots. A lawyer called O'Hare put up an extraordinary proposal that there should be a pitched battle to decide the issue, thirty loyalists and thirty Orangemen being picked from either side 'to determine the matter by a general scrimmage.' But since this free fight was not to take place until after the Prince had left, it did not seem to offer an immediate solution. It was therefore decided that the Prince should sail. The Orangemen, sensitive that for once the other side were called loyalists, assembled on the quay and gave three cheers for Queen Victoria, three cheers for Garibaldi (who was then engaged in the liberation of Italy), and three groans for the Duke of Newcastle.

The Prince of Wales then intervened in the councils of war with his own shrewd human diplomacy. He was aware that he was already the idol of the ladies of Canada, and thought that perhaps they could use their influence on the menfolk. He was due at a town called Coburg, and had already twice declined to go to a ball there. Now he said that he would dance at the ball, if he landed. Masculine politics could not stand up against the feminine rush for the bait. There was no Orange display at Coburg. Instead, fifty gentlemen assembled on the wharf after dinner, all carrying torches, and they drew the Prince from the ship to the ballroom by ropes attached to his carriage. The Prince of Wales danced all night, and the way was smoother for the entry into Toronto.

He arrived by special train on a Saturday, in pouring rain again, which actually eased the situation, since all out-door celebrations had to be postponed until the Monday. Newcastle had been active in insisting on the removal of all Orange arches, but one arch remained after its dismantling had been forcibly resisted, and the Prince had to drive under it on his way to Government House. Newcastle sent for the Mayor and lashed him in language so extreme that the Mayor refused to apologize, so Newcastle banned the Corporation from attending the Prince's levée. Edward again applied his tact. He had noticed the Orange arch, covered with the colours and insignia of the Order, before the Duke of Newcastle, and his reaction was not pompous. He called out, laughing, 'You're caught at last, Duke. You have got to go under Uncle William now!'

On the next day, however, there broke out the most serious rioting of the tour. The Orange arch stood in King Street, on the Prince's route to church. The Duke of Newcastle insisted that it should be taken down, but because of his unhappy relations with the Mayor he was unsuccessful. Newcastle therefore ordered the coachman to take another road to the church and this provoked more trouble:

> ... the vast concourse of people, disappointed and angry, showered curses and maledictions on the sandy-covered pate of his stubborn Grace. While the Prince was in church, where the audience jostled and squeezed in the most ill-mannered way, the crowd outside and near the arch grew to the proportions of a mob. They hooted and yelled, calling out all manner of insulting language. The principal men of the Orange lodge brought down their most emphatic insignia, and in a short time the arch displayed the banners and flags which are generally carried in

The Orange Arches at Toronto caused the most serious rioting of the tour of Canada.

their processions. One banner, on which was a picture of King William, the names of the principal Orange battle-fields, and appropriate mottoes, was hung so low that had the Prince's carriage passed under it, it would have wiped his nose.

The mob, acting under the advice of their leaders, made a rush to the Prince's carriage, intending to take the horses from it and compel the Prince to go under the arch. When the Prince came out, some called to bring him up and make him go under the arch—force him under—while others cheered and some hooted.

The Prince became pale, and turned from the Governor to the Duke, as if asking counsel. The Duke, stern and determined, strode ahead. The police cleared the way, and the royal party were again seated when the mob gathered round the horses. By order of the Duke, the coachman plied his whip. The horses reared and plunged. And to the great danger of those to the front the cortège passed swiftly through, while mingled cheers, groans and hisses followed them.

This was the climax of the trouble, and from then the heat ran steadily down. The Mayor and Corporation of Toronto apologized to the Prince, and he held a special levée for their attendance. He also received deputations from Kingston and from Belleville who expressed their regrets for the poor welcome extended to him. Edward assured them that he bore no grudge, and he would tell the Queen of their sincerity. The Mayor of Kingston thanked him 'in a voice half choked with sobs', Possibly Newcastle's correct but intransigent stand had been due to a misunderstanding of the legal position of the Orange movement. At that time Canada was more liberal than the United Kingdom: party processions of either militant Catholics or Protestants were not illegal there, although they were then in Ireland.

The Prince passed on. The last lap in Canada was the road to Niagara. The deluge of loyal addresses continued. On the way, while an address was being read, two little girls made their way to the dais, and one of them put a bouquet of flowers in his hand. 'She was rewarded by an audible "Thank you, sissy" and a sweet smile. A terrible ordeal was then prepared for the Prince, who listened to four addresses, to which he gave written replies.'

Edward had reached the end of his tether, and was more than ready for a few days' rest at Niagara. On the night before he got there the observant Press reported: 'The Prince is really quite exhausted. He falls asleep everywhere, and was only kept awake at dinner yesterday by frequent experiments with snuff, the taking of which makes him sneeze like a baby.' At Niagara he stayed at Clifton House, in the grounds of which trees had been trimmed to improve his view of the Falls. Over the gateway was yet another

Blondin above Niagara Falls for the personal thrill of the Prince of Wales. As a unique climax he re-crossed the wire on stilts.

triumphal arch. But this time it was not political, having been made by old Robinson, formerly superintendent of the garden at Aber-geldie, near Balmoral, at that time belonging to Victoria's mother, the Duchess of Kent, and soon to be taken over by Edward. The arch, thirty feet high, was 'adorned with representations of forest scenery and American life, and surmounted at the summit by a splendid stuffed deer in the attitude of flight with upreared head and lofty antlers.'

The Prince relaxed for an evening, contenting himself with the view of the Falls from the house, after Niagara had been illumi-nated for the first time in history, using two hundred of the largest Bengal lights. Next day he went to watch the French acrobat Blondin cross the Falls on a tightrope. Blondin's act included a great number of crossings; taking a man across in a wheelbarrow, carrying one on his back, standing on his head on the tight-rope and turning somersaults. Edward went to congratulate him:

> Blondin announced to the Prince that in his honor he would do what he
> had never before done in public—cross on stilts. The Prince remons-
> trated, and said that he was entirely satisfied, and did not wish him to
> endanger himself on his account. But Blondin reassured him. Finally he
> offered, in the most gentlemanly way, to carry the Prince over. And had
> it not been for the Duke there is no telling what might have been the
> result of the interview.

Edward had, in fact, accepted the offer, but conceded to the pleas
of Newcastle. So Blondin put on stilts and made a final crossing
'although it was with very great difficulty and with infinite pain to
all beholders.' Edward later sent Blondin a purse of sixty
sovereigns—a fair Prince's ransom.

The Prince recovered his energy and spirits speedily, and entirely
delighted the Americans, who were now his growing escort as they
prepared to take him their side of the border. Howard of the *New
York Times* fancied that he saw blossoming in him the true spirit of
Young America:

> The ball this evening was a fine affair. It was largely attended, and
> honored by the presence of the Prince, who is fast becoming a great
> favourite with the Americans. Since his quiet rest here he has picked up
> wonderfully. At the ball he was very free, and entered into the
> enjoyments of the evening with an evident relish. Whether it is the
> proximity of the Land of the Free, or the superabundance of pretty
> American girls who have flocked hither in swarms, I cannot pretend to
> say.
>   But it is a certainty that the Prince has exhibited more of the quality
> termed 'Young America' within the past few days than in all his trip
> before. Tommy [*ie* Englishman] must look to his laurels.

At Windsor, Ontario, the Prince of Wales boarded the Detroit
and Milwaukie Ferry, and instantly became Baron Renfrew, a
private person, for he was not visiting the United States as foreign
royalty. When the steamer reached American waters, Mayor Bahl of
Detroit, who was already on board the ferryboat, bade him welcome
to the United States. Ahead of them ranged in the river for the
length of a mile, was a large fleet of river and lake vessels rigged
with lights and banners. As the steamer passed through, each of the
welcoming vessels sent up a shower of rockets and fireworks.
Thirty thousand people were waiting to greet Edward on the
Woodward Avenue waterfront. The city militia and the fire brigade
were on parade with torches, but their force was not sufficient to
get him through unshaken by the hand or unbeaten on the back.

This rapturous welcome was to be the rule for the next three weeks.

Edward responded in the highest spirits, and accepted the naivetés of super-republicans. At Chicago a millionaire called Sturgis, said to be more wealthy than wise, remarked when he was introduced, 'Lord Renfrew, eh! But you're no better than anybody else. I shall call you Mr Renfrew.' And he did so through the entire visit.

From Chicago Edward went to Dwight, then a small village on the prairie, where he shot a hundred quail, and other game birds. He then began an extensive tour, by way of St Louis and Cincinnati to Pittsburgh, where his rail-car was mobbed by 10,000 people cheering themselves hoarse until he was energetically waving his hat high above his head. After Baltimore he came to Washington. President James Buchanan received him like a father—they had met when Buchanan was Ambassador in London—and his pretty niece, Harriet Lane, was appropriately cousinly. But by now Edward was being reported as 'making himself agreeable to many a fair damsel'. After days of sightseeing, he came on to Philadelphia, which he thought the most attractive city in the States. One of its attractions was a bathroom suite in his apartment at the Continental Hotel. 'The Prince delights in a morning bath—a luxury which he has not at all times lately been able to enjoy.' Philadelphia's other model feature was its prison, which Edward visited. Entering the cell of the former Judge Vandersmith, convicted for corruption and forgery, Edward asked if there was any objection to a conversation. 'Talk away, Prince,' said the Judge. 'There's time enough—I'm here for twenty years.'

The way was clear for New York, which Edward entered by sea, but not in a ship of the Royal Navy. There were not only political difficulties about the British Fleet calling at New York, but it was feared that the delights of the city would entice many Jack Tars to desert. The Prince (his incognito was in shreds by now) landed at the Battery and reviewed troops there, in the full uniform of a Colonel and wearing the Order of the Garter. He then made perhaps the most acclaimed trip down Broadway which that street had yet witnessed. Seated beside Mayor Fernando Wood in a specially-built barouche, he was cheered by 200,000 people in the street, and throngs in every window; every Broadway hotel parlour facing the street, had been booked ten days in advance. From City Hall, Edward drove to the Fifth Avenue Hotel, which he declared more comfortable than Buckingham Palace. It also attracted its share of cranks as did the Palace. As the Prince left his hotel for a later engagement a sailor rushed up to him shouting, 'You never shall be King of England, not if you live a hundred years.' Police removed the man and put him up before Justice Connolly, who promptly discharged him after a reprimand. He was ascertained to be an Englishman, Edward Moncar, second mate of a ship curiously named the *Santa Claus,* who 'entertained a strong antipathy to monarchical governments and their representatives.'

Some newspapers blew up this incident as an attempted assassination. The *New York Times* described it as an assault. The paper promptly received an indignant post-card from Mr Edward Moncar, which it printed unamended:

> Mr Editor i saw in your saturday issue that i am accused of an assault on the Prince of wales which is false i mearly said what i thought and i think so still that he never will be King of england if he Lives for a 100 years time for Kings is gorn and i Pointed the finger of scorn at the baby faced english man as they gaunted him along and now appeal to Americans to know weather it is Constitutionall to Pay homage to a Prince if so i am Done if not then why was i seased Like a felin by a Lot of what Dogs Dressed in uniform for they acted Like such as soon as i opened my Mouth i am not a tinker or a tailor But i am what i am and that is what i Did not see many of on that Day that is i Mean a true republican and i am glad to find that Justice Connolly and i Drunk of one spirit
>
> Edward Moncar

The Prince of Wales perused this eloquent defence as, in some pain, he recovered from the effects of the great ball given in his honour at the New York Academy of Music. Three thousand tickets had been issued for this event. The urge to get in was so great that the Black Market price for a ticket was 250 dollars, and it was certain that far more than the calculated number finally, by one means or another, gained the coveted prize of entry. The description of the ball in the flower-decked academy began in a suitably florid fashion:

> All that music could do to enchant an aromatic atmosphere with melody, the most superb bands procurable in America abundantly did. The Prince of Wales, who apparently has Queen Elizabeth's passion for dancing, made his entrée punctually at ten o'clock. The stately Mrs Morgan [wife of the Governor of New York] in a cloud of crape alive with diamonds was at her post, prepared to open the ball as became the queen regnant of the Empire State, with the young heir of England. And yet, at midnight, the ball had not begun. 'Someone had blundered'.

The blunder in organization had, in fact, been serious. They had let so many people into the ball that the floor collapsed before the

first dance. The Prince and Queen Morgan retreated to the supper room while carpenters tried to repair the floor, but nobody danced for hours, and the crush was so great that every ball gown blended into 'one undistinguishable mass of splendour'.

The Prince had additional memories and discomforts. 'The poor youth is literally covered with black and blue spots. Women who had given up all hope of being introduced to him pushed him, punched him, pinched him, jostled him, squeezed his arm when they thought they could do so unobserved. . . .' Edward had had his baptism of fire for his subsequent visits to West Point and Bunker's Hill. At Boston the pressure was eased, and he was given what he said was the most enjoyable ball of his stay, before sailing in the *Hero* from Portland, Maine on a storm-tossed return voyage that took twenty-six days.

Edward's parents welcomed him, but his father commented that he was late for his term at Oxford. Edward went dutifully to Oxford, of which even Queen Victoria disapproved, for most un-Victorian reasons, as 'that old monkish place which I have a horror of.' But the Prince of Wales was at the end of his monkish days.

The race for Alexandra

WHILE Edward had been extending his personality in America there had been much thought at home about whom to pair him off with. Candidates for marriage to the heir to the throne of Great Britain had to be RHASP— Royal, Healthy, Anglo-Saxon, Protestant.[1] Surprisingly only nine young women could be considered, and there were serious objections to all of them on various grounds: their stupidity, their youth, their dowdiness, their mothers. In such a dismal market, decent dressing was welcomed but good looks were virtually despaired of 'Beauty is rare,' said one of the match-makers—a pleasant person, but no oil-painting herself—'and not really a necessity, only a pleasant gingerbread.' And she renewed her desperate search through the pages of the *Almanach de Gotha*.

However, one beauty was eventually put forward as a dark mare. While Edward was storm-tossed in the Atlantic aboard HMS *Hero* out of Portland, a portentous dinner-party was given at Windsor Castle. The bride of the British Minister in Copenhagen, formerly a lady-in-waiting to Edward's elder sister Vicky, who had married the heir to the throne of Prussia, proposed to the Prince Consort the name of Princess Alexandra of Schleswig-Holstein-Sonderburg-Glucksburg. She was not quite sixteen, the eldest daughter of Prince Christian of that house. Prince Christian had been approved some eight years earlier by Great Britain, Russia, France, Prussia, Austria and Sweden as successor to King Frederick VII of Denmark, an alcoholic roué of a character deplorable even by European Royal standards, who had divorced two wives and was living in morganatic marriage with a woman of doubtful reputation. He had been reliably declared impotent, which made it advisable to secure the succession, and, although it is true and characteristic that none of the High Contracting Parties actually consulted the Danish people, Prince Christian's rivals were not nationally popular since they all espoused one or other of the wrong sides in the Schleswig-Holstein Question. This political question was the running sore of Danish life. The country had already lost eighty-five per cent of its former territory by ceding independence to Norway. The separation of the southern Duchies of Schleswig and Holstein was now being sought by two opposing forces, the nationalism of Holstein and the imperialism of Prussia. The loss of this territory

---

1 'Anglo-Saxon' is as superstitious and arbitrary a term as 'Nordic' and, like the Nazi term, was intended to exclude Slavs and Latins. But European royalty was not particularly native, and in the nineteenth century the thrones of Belgium, Portugal, Spain (even Mexico), Rumania, Bulgaria, Yugo-Slavia, Greece, as well as Great Britain, Germany, Russia, Sweden, Norway, and Denmark, were occupied by descendants of King George III of Great Britain. Some sovereigns changed their religion to Roman or Orthodox Catholic.

would mean that the country would be diminished by well over a third of its remaining area.

Prince Christian therefore was recognized as royal because of his political designation as heir to a throne. His daughter was more indubitably royal because of her descent, through her mother, from a line of Landgraves of Hesse-Cassel—but of the Hesse-Cassels, in Victoria's Court, the less said the better: they were considered a fast lot. Edward and Alexandra were in fact fourth cousins, each being a great-great-great-grandchild of King George II of Great Britain.

It was also a fact that Alexandra was a conspicuously poor relation. The one reform of drunken King Frederick VII for which the Danes still honour him was that he democratized the country. This brought Alexandra no comfort. Her father had had to live for years on his pay as an army captain, and even as heir to the throne his allowances amounted to only £2000 a year, about two per cent of Edward's. This did not spoil Alexandra's girlhood. She merely got used to making her own clothes. It did affect her extravagance in later life. She was one of the few people who never handled money, first in poverty, then in wealth, and she literally never knew the value of it.

The first physical reports on Alexandra, given to a dubious Victoria and Albert, were that she was tall (by Victoria's standard—Alexandra was five foot three) with very pretty features, 'a lovely figure but very thin', and was 'most ladylike and aristocratic.' She had been brought up by English nurses and, besides Danish, spoke English, French and German, in that order, as it subsequently appeared, for she did not favour German for a number of psychological reasons. Like Edward, she spoke English with a marked accent.

Queen Victoria hardly bothered to consider Alexandra's qualities. She rejected her as a possible daughter-in-law on two counts. The first was her Danish connection, which was inconvenient to Victoria and to the British Foreign Office, since it was rightly anticipated that the imminent death of the dissolute King Frederick would raise the Schleswig-Holstein question, upon which Victoria supported Prussia, and the Foreign Office saw no material advantage in supporting Denmark.[1] The second objection was the descent of Alexandra's mother from the house of Hesse-Cassel, and her continuing connection with what was, in her eyes, a not-too-respectable family. The reality seems to be that this family, from which George

1 In imperialist thinking, this was short-sighted. Disregarding local nationalist sentiment, Prussia wanted Schleswig-Holstein in order to construct the Kiel Canal and give her Baltic-based navy access to the North Sea. The eventual construction of this canal was a major strategic disadvantage to Great Britain in two world wars.

'From that photograph I would marry her at once,' said Prince Albert, inspecting pictures of Alexandra which were witheld from Edward.

V's consort Queen Mary sprang, was unruly, jolly, but only reprehensible for being decidedly un-Albertian. They came together in the summer at their holiday home at Rumpenheim Castle, and went a bit wild: Alexandra used to go there and, though she was a tomboy, they once shocked her with their goings-on, as will be seen. But their principle sin, in Victoria's eyes, was that they were anti-Prussian.

So Victoria and Albert rejected Alexandra outright. But within a few days they heard that there were rivals for her hand, which raised her market value. The Emperor of Russia, Alexander II, had asked his secret service to secure photographs of Alexandra, since he was considering annexing her for his own heir. In addition, scouts were out in Copenhagen on behalf of the Prince of Orange, already a wild youth, whose private life was later to become a public scandal. Edward was still on the high seas. Would his fate be sealed while he was powerless to intervene?

Victoria sacrificed a pawn of self-pride in a queen's gambit directed at her daughter in Prussia. Vicky was instructed to submit photographs of Alexandra. The effect of these was explosive. Albert said, 'From that photograph I would marry her at once!' Victoria said, 'The one of Princess Alexandra is indeed lovely! What a pity she is who she is!' Albert, on second thoughts, said, 'We take the Princess, but not her relations.' Victoria, inserting the wedge, insisted that her son's choice must still lie between two German princesses. 'The beauty of Denmark is much against our wishes. I do wish somebody would go and marry her off—at once. If Bertie could see and like one of the others first than I am sure we should be safe.'

Edward was home now, and in order to advance this plan the photographs of Alexandra were hidden from him. 'Bertie shall not see one of them. That must not be.' More pictures of the German candidates were requested, but these ladies were candidly admitted to be more intellectual than beautiful, and Bertie's taste in women was already clearly recognized, along with the dire results of a match that did not satisfy that taste. 'I think of our English ladies and how much Bertie admires them,' moaned his sister. 'And oh, what use would cleverness be—without some attractions to captivate him, all the influence of a clever wife would be gone if he did not care about her.'

In desperation Victoria found herself forced to give instructions that further enquiries should be made about Alexandra: 'whether she is clever, quiet, not frivolous or vain.' With one blow of her bludgeon she knocked out the poor girl's parents: 'The mother's family are bad—the father's foolish.' And she urged accuracy and speed in the investigation which was 'so very important with the peculiar character we have to deal with'. This was a side-swipe at her son Edward, who had come home and speedily out worn the praise he had won for his American success. After keeping four terms at Oxford he was now at Cambridge, minding his own business and only seeing his parents when he was commanded to make the cross-country journey to Windsor for a theatrical performance in the Castle. Yet he still managed to irritate his mother.

This exasperation grew so marked during the Easter Vacation of 1861 that Vicky, who had come over from Berlin to rejoin the family, begged her mother, whose character she could candidly

assess, not to promote an estrangement with Bertie. Victoria made no practical response except to work herself up into a state of neurotic tension until her son left the palace: 'His voice made me so nervous I could hardly bear it.' But during the family reunion Edward had learned from his sister Vicky, with whom he was always affectionately intimate, of the tentative plans that were being pursued on his behalf; and for the first time he knew who Alexandra was. As soon as Edward had left home his father confirmed the marriage project in writing. The Prince Consort had the peculiar characteristic of doing everything by memo, as if he could not speak openly and intimately within his family. Even when Victoria had had one of her frequent colossal rows with him he would retire for twenty-four hours and send her a letter detailing every stage of the quarrel and explaining how it was impossible for him at the time to counter the mounting illogicality of her outbursts. These letters are a fascinating and accurate documentation of the behaviour of a wife who is determined to quarrel with her husband at all costs, and their detail is invaluable for historians, but they also expose a painful lack of ease within the family of Victoria and Albert.

Albert told his son that, if Edward did become interested in Alexandra, all objections to her family would be overcome and any

Czar Alexander II of Russia, the hunter from whom Princess Alexandra had to be preserved — though he was later allowed to snatch Alix's younger sister Dagmar.

Vicky, Edward's elder sister and Victoria's most intimate daughter, Crown Princess of Prussia and briefly Victoria, Empress of Germany, pulled off an espionage coup to get a credible report on Alexandra's rating as a bride for Edward.

74

diplomatic obstacle surmounted. He mentioned a verbal agreement that Albert and Edward had already come to, that Edward had better get married early, a conclusion apparently reached as the very reason for marriage which Victoria struck out of the Marriage Service: 'for a remedy against sin, and to avoid fornication; that such persons as have not the gift of continency might marry.'

Meanwhile, as anxiety mounted over the intentions of the Russian Emperor, who was skilfully stalking Alexandra, Vicky pulled off a great coup of espionage. She set her English nursemaid to pump another nursemaid in the Prussian Royal Family, after learning that the second nurse had been with Alexandra for ten years. The intelligence report read like a glowing recommendation: the subject was strong, healthy, had never had any illness but measles, and, in short, was 'the sweetest girl who ever lived—and full of life and spirits.'

On the extraordinary basis of this servants' gossip, Victoria dropped her reserve and went overboard for Alexandra, seeing the match as a victory to be won over the Czar of Russia as the final campaign in the inconclusive Crimean War. She concurred with Vicky's enthusiastic jingoism: 'It would be dreadful if this pearl went to the horrid Russians.'

In the Long Vacation, Edward left Cambridge for a short and concentrated command course in the Army, serving with the Grenadier Guards in camp at the Curragh, County Kildare, outside Dublin. He was naturally irked that he was given the status of a brigadier before he had the skill to drill a company, and was compelled to spend many of his evenings entertaining senior officers. But he did attend occasional regimental guest-nights, and he made enthusiastic efforts to mix as much as possible with brother officers of his own age. In generous recompense and recognition that the Prince was really trying to be one of them, some young officers gallantly put an actress into his bed as treasure trove for the Prince to discover when he came back from the mess.

The girl was Nellie Clifden, and Edward fell in love with her. He liked her so much that, with considerable skill—for he had to dodge the personal supervision of his Governor and equerries—he brought her back to England and installed her in lodgings at Windsor. But unfortunately the mechanics of his match-making had been advanced to the stage when Edward was due to go to Europe and make an inspection of Princess Alexandra. He could not avoid this, and went to Germany. Nellie Clifden went to London, and talked too boastfully.

In an understandable emotional whirl, Edward went to Speyer, near Heidelberg, and, in front of an altar at the cathedral there, met Alexandra who, by an 'accident' arranged by Vicky, was visiting the cathedral at the same time. They talked for a quarter of an hour, and that night Edward met Alexandra's parents who, by another accident, were staying at the same hotel as Edward and Vicky. Alexandra's family was due to return to their holiday castle at Rumpenheim where, her mother conceded, the atmosphere was a little free, particularly as inspired by Edward's cousin, Princess Mary of Cambridge. She said Mary's conversation was not fit for young girls, and she had seen Mary flirting so outrageously that she had told Alexandra, 'If you ever become such a coquette as Mary you will get a box on the ears', to which Alexandra had tactfully replied that she would deserve it.

Edward and Alexandra exchanged signed photographs at Heidelberg, and parted. Edward wrote fairly non-committally to his mother, 'I thought her charming and very pretty'. He was due in Scotland, but gave himself time for a night in London before reaching Balmoral. Vicky had already reported to her mother that 'Alix has made an impression on Bertie, though in his own funny and undemonstrative way'—a typical reaction from a pressurized young man within his family, since 'undemonstrative' was not a word used often about Edward. Victoria retorted, more sourly, that 'as for being in love, I don't think he can be, or that he is capable of enthusiasm about anything in the world.'

Victoria and Albert now began to put more pressure on their reluctant heir. Victoria discovered with horror that Bertie had developed 'a sudden fear of marrying and above all of having children'. She thought this a strange fear in so young a man, yet it is very common among ignorant innocents who imagine that their first fornication may have given them a disease. Albert, still incapable of man-to-man communication, penned another of his extraordinarily stiff memos, a recital of grievances which might have been despatched to a son serving in Timbuctoo, though in reality Edward was lounging in the next room. He reminded Bertie that he had agreed to marry early because 'it would be impossible for you to lead, with any chance of success or comfort to yourself, a protracted bachelor life.' The family had gone to great lengths to arrange a meeting with Alexandra, but Edward now asked that the princess and her parents should be invited to Windsor for a further meeting. If Victoria and Albert conceded this, which does not seem, on objective consideration, an unreasonable request or a damaging concession, then Edward must understand that he must propose marriage immediately or release the already compromised Alexandra.

John Brown with Queen
Victoria. 'May you have
no deaths in the family,'
he wished her with failing
foresight just before the
Prince Consort and two
kinsmen died of typhoid.

The visit was approved. Edward went back to Cambridge. Victoria left Balmoral, and was given a peculiar and portentous farewell by her Highland servant, John Brown, who hoped they would have a safe winter 'and, above all, that you may have no deaths in the family'. On the same day, from his den in Germany, the decrepit Baron Stockmar, once the confidential adviser of both Victoria and Albert and still anxious to insert his finger and stir a muddy pie, launched a double-forked blasting on the reputation of Edward and the completion of any marriage-contract with Alexandra.

He disclosed the affair of the Prince of Wales with Nellie Clifden. This was the first that the parents had heard of it, gossip flowing faster towards Stockmar than to them, and Albert immediately started investigations to confirm it. Then Stockmar advanced hypocritical and lying arguments against the marriage. It was conceived in the hope, he said, that the moral qualities of Alexandra would counter-balance the conspicuous lack of morality in the Prince of Wales (after one affair!). But there was no guarantee of morality in Alexandra. Alexandra's father was an imbecile and her mother was a lustful intriguer whose present family had not all been sired by her husband. Stockmar had already circulated or confirmed the Nellie Clifden scandal to interested royalties in Europe. He disingenuously hoped it would go no farther, because the disgusting facts already compelled every honourable man to cry out: 'Not a step farther, or we shall acquiesce in a disaster of unparalleled impact.'

It is difficult to find an equal to such a poisonous, canting and perjured intervention. To clear the falsehoods now, in anticipation of the immense work that was done to investigate them, it can be stated that Alexandra's father was not an imbecile, and although Victoria, on his visit of approval before the marriage, registered him as 'not bright', he served as a reasonably efficient king after six Powers had nominated him for the throne. Alexandra's mother did not have an illegitimate child nor had the princess herself, as Stockmar suggested, coquetted so heavily that young officers concerned had been dismissed from Copenhagen, but an illegitimate child had been borne by Alexandra's aunt, whose daughter had started the gossip to divert attention from her mother.

The immediate impact of Stockmar's elephantine interference was on young Edward. Albert swiftly found confirmation of the Nellie Clifden story, which was already stale in London Society. He communicated with his son, again not face to face, but by letter. He said that he was too heart-broken to confront his son, and he did not even want a personal letter in reply. But Edward was to confess everything to his governor, General Bruce, who would relay the sordid story to the Prince Consort.

To incite his son to proper horror and repentance, Albert painted an extreme hell-fire picture of the situation as he saw it. This composition was the neurotic production of a sick man stricken in his most vulnerable zone, the management of the sex impulse. After declaring that the Prince of Wales was already the laughing-stock of the profligates of London, Albert speculated with horror on a possible outcome of the affair which did not, in fact, then materialize, but which was surprisingly closely paralleled some years later. This was the possibility, as Albert dreaded it, that Nellie Clifden might take Edward to the law court on a paternity suit and give 'disgusting details' of his behaviour before handing him over for cross-examination by a 'railing indecent attorney'.

Edward was still a very impressionable lad, with a sincere respect for his father's feelings, and he admitted with an appealing simplicity that there had been an impulsive affair, and that emotionally it had meant something to him, but he declared that it had ended. This was reported back to Windsor. The Prince Consort replied, in a further letter, that he accepted this and there would be no more recriminations. But he declared that the whole episode emphasized the urgent necessity that Edward should conclude an early marriage to save himself, Great Britain and the world from perdition—which was a dramatically high price to put on the consequences of a few bachelor indiscretions.

Albert decided that he could now endure the ordeal of actually seeing his son, and he went to Cambridge for the interview. The meeting was unexpectedly successful, although, in exaggerating for penitential purposes the alleged effect of the episode on Victoria, Albert deceived his son. Initially it had been the sexually delicate Prince Consort who was far more shocked than the Queen. However, man to man, Albert and Edward went for a long walk on a wretched November day, and talked all night in amity. Possibly a basis had been laid for a far more trusting relationship in the future. But Edward was never to speak to his father again.

Albert was incubating typhoid fever and already showing the symptoms. Victoria preferred to believe, and never in her forty remaining years banished the resentment from her heart, that he had been struck down by the shock of his son's affair with an actress. During the November of the 'exposure', Edward's youngest brother Leopold, who was always weak from haemophilia, was worryingly ill, and two Saxe-Coburg kinsmen to whom the Prince Consort was devoted—King Pedro of Portugal and his brother Prince Ferdinand—died in a typhoid epidemic which ravaged the Portuguese Court. John Brown's morbid exorcism against 'deaths in the family', which always impressed Queen Victoria, had failed, and the disaster was crowned with the death of Prince Albert on 14 December 1861. Queen Victoria had vindictively refused to summon the Prince of Wales from Cambridge, and he arrived only in the last dawn, after a private message from his sister Alice, to hear the death-rattle.

Victoria stolidly maintained to her statesmen and her family that Edward had killed his father: 'There must be no illusion about that—it was so; he was struck down—and I never can see Bertie without a shudder.' She decided on two immediate objectives. 'Marry early Bertie must . . . a nice wife that he likes, she will keep him straight.' And there seemed no alternative to Alexandra, provided that she was accepted as a pliant tool by Victoria herself. 'I should see the girl before Bertie sees her again so that I could judge, before it is too late, *whether she will suit me*', declared this formidable matriarch.

But, since a long period of mourning must ensue before a marriage, the Prince of Wales must be sent away, out of the country, on a four-and-a-half-month tour of the Middle East and the Holy Land. And at Calvary he had better remember his mother. 'It was so. He was struck down. I never can see Bertie without a shudder. Oh! that bitterness. Oh! that cross!'

Bertie himself was not unwilling to go, and so stop making his mother shudder. He enjoyed himself, and clearly got over his emotional tangle, for he cheerfully accepted the fact that Nellie Clifden was now the plaything of Lord Carrington, at the age of eighteen a precocious member of Edward's set whom he had left behind at Cambridge, and who was to inherit, in his career, more than one of Edward's discarded mistresses.

Meanwhile Victoria set about clearing the imbroglio over Alexandra. She sorted out the false reports of the imbecility and immorality of Prince and Princess Christian of Schleswig-Holstein-Sonderburg-Glucksburg. She resolutely faced the Russian threat. The Czar was casting his net wider to include Alexandra's younger sister Dagmar as an alternative bride for his heir. Vicky reported from Berlin that Alexandra's mother was feeling very

The age of gloom is officially ushered in by the funeral of Edward's father, Albert the Prince Consort, killed, according to Queen Victoria, by shock at their son's immorality. It was Edward's rôle to refute the doom and the gloom.

nervous in case the touring Bertie did not eventually ask for Alexandra's hand, and to meet that possibility she was not discouraging the Czar since 'she would still wish to have the Cesarewitch in reserve.' In the meantime, said Vicky, it was to be hoped that the Czarevitch would not fall for Dagmar 'as it would be one chance less for Affie' (Prince Alfred, later Duke of Edinburgh, Edward's younger brother, then aged seventeen). Victoria, however, said that if Bertie did not take Alexandra 'Affie would be ready to take her at once,' though Victoria would insist on a three-year engagement. As for Dagmar, 'I do not wish her to be kept for Affie. Let the Emperor have her.'

Unfortunately Affie soon lost favour with his mother, for, celebrating his eighteenth birthday, he got involved in a scandal of his own which Victoria blasted as 'heartless and dishonourable . . . Affie's conduct is far worse than Bertie's.' Victoria was, indeed, compelled to support Bertie when gossiping German relations not only reported the Nellie Clifden episode, ten months late, to Alexandra's parents—in their Copenhagen backwater the news had not reached them before—but also added the damaging rider that the Queen and the Prince of Wales were at daggers drawn. Consequently Princess Christian feared that Alexandra would be unhappy in England because Victoria's hatred of Edward would be transferred to his wife.

'Let Princess Christian know', thundered the Queen in a tissue of loyal lying, 'that wicked wretches had led our poor boy into a scrape which had caused his beloved father and myself the deepest pain, but that both of us had forgiven him this (one) sad mistake, that we had never disagreed, and that I was very confident that he would make a steady husband.'

Next, Victoria had to deal with a further German canard. Stockmar, stonewalled on his imbecility accusation, now said that Alexandra had a mark on her neck caused by scrofula. The tuberculous affection known as scrofula would be a serious objection to a bride claiming RHASP qualifications, since her future health would be suspect. Victoria exercised herself and obtained the best possible evidence that the mark was 'nothing whatever but a cold on which a stupid doctor had tried experiments.' (Alexandra herself was always self-conscious about the blemish on her neck, and she introduced the massive jewelled choker or dog-collar, which became highly characteristic of her, and widely copied as a fashion.)

It was now time for Victoria to examine Alexandra and have her delivered on approval. She chose to do this in a peculiar series of arrangements. She met Prince and Princess Christian, with Alexandra, during a day passed at the palace of the King of the Belgians, at Laeken outside Brussels. She moved on immediately to demonstrate her devotion to her dead husband by revisiting Coburg. The Prince of Wales was then called up to pass a day with Alexandra at Ostend and a further day at Laeken, where he proposed and was accepted. He was then given five days to cultivate the acquaintance in a room next to that of Alexandra's mother, for short periods only, and on Victoria's insistence, with the door open. The Queen then demanded three weeks of Alexandra's continuous company, in absolute solitude, at Windsor. To make sure that she received undivided attention, she banished Edward on an unwanted Mediterranean cruise, and complained bitterly when she saw that his letters to Alexandra were all written in English, when 'the German element is the one I wish to be cherished and kept up in our beloved home.'

If Alexandra had not 'suited her' during this probationary period, it would have been dangerously late for Victoria to halt the marriage. But, as it turned out, the Queen was full of praise and ambition for her future daughter-in-law, and fixed the wedding for the soonest practicable date, which happened to fall in the middle of Lent. When the Church authorities objected, citing the rules of abstinence, Victoria boomed back, 'Marriage is a solemn holy act *not* to be classed with amusements.' No one was going to suggest publicly to *her* that sexual intercourse was a pleasure.

There were three months of preparation. There seems no doubt,

Victoria inspected the parents of her son's prospective bride at the Royal Palace in Brussels.

since Edward was of an age to want to be in love, that he fell in love with complete abandon and, expressing that feeling, covered many hundreds of pages of writing-paper which were later, by order, burned. He made his plans to set up home at Marlborough House in Pall Mall, and at the newly acquired Norfolk mansion of Sandringham. Edward had come of age during his enforced Mediterranean cruise. He now found that he had an income of about £100,000 a year, half coming from his inheritance of the Duchy of Cornwall and half from a Parliamentary grant. In addition he had private capital of about half a million pounds. Alexandra got a Parliamentary grant of £10,000 a year 'pin-money', which was five times her father's total allowance for keeping up appearances as heir to the throne of Denmark.

And so they were married, on 10 March 1864, amid a confusion of circumstances which was worthy of a black farce. The Queen was determined on an atmosphere of ostentatious gloom. The public wanted a party. They had endured fifteen months of imposed national mourning. They felt a need to celebrate a corporate loyalty and affection. Rejected by the Queen, the common people transferred their goodwill to the Prince of Wales and his bride (with comparatively little basis and no prompting, for the art of public relations was not then efficiently practised by the Court, and in any case was officially diverted from 'that wretched boy'). With remarkable spontaneity the ordinary citizens of Margate, of Gravesend, of London, as well as the uncommon schoolboys of Eton, came out *en masse* to welcome Alexandra on her entry into England, and London Society crammed the bow-windows of Piccadilly to watch the Prince and Princess pass by on their way to Windsor.

Queen Victoria had stipulated that the marriage must take place in the privacy of St George's Chapel instead of publicly in London, and even insisted on half-mourning dress to be worn by the royal guests. With ghoulish obsession she first took Edward and Alexandra to the mausoleum of the Prince Consort. She joined their hands before his tomb, and declared with dramatic intensity, 'He gives you his blessing.' On the wedding day she insisted that a photograph be taken which remains as possibly the most repulsive picture in the Royal Archives. It shows Alexandra looking helpless, Edward looking chinlessly resentful, and Victoria wearing full mourning, in profile, gazing with theatrical piety at the bust of her dead husband.

And yet there was the bustle of heraldry, bright uniforms, sparkling diamonds—one duchess wore half a million pounds worth of jewellery at the wedding—thirty-six royal guests and a suffoca-

'The most repulsive
picture in the Royal
Archives' — the
wedding-day photograph
on which Victoria
insisted.

tion of aristocracy. It was a great occasion, which might perhaps have been expected to overawe a penurious Danish princess of eighteen who had previously done her own dressmaking. Yet she had the fire to declare to Vicky, Crown Princess of Prussia, before the ceremony, 'You may think I like marrying Bertie for his position, but if he were a cowboy I would love him just the same, and would marry no one else.' And Alexandra jauntily laid the foundation of a reputation for massive unpunctuality which she was to observe for sixty years: she was ten minutes late at the altar. She was later to establish a par of half-an-hour extra on that first maidenly precedent.

After a brief honeymoon, Edward and Alexandra inaugurated the first of a revolutionary new series of brilliant Society seasons, re-introducing an opulent glamour at their 'alternative Court' at Marlborough House. Queen Victoria looked on with disapproval. Within a month she was moaning at Bertie's gay behaviour and at the late nights the couple were keeping. An even more disturbing alarm was sounded by the realization that Edward's brother Affie, at eighteen was dangerously attracted to Alexandra. 'We do all we can to keep him from Marlborough House as he is far too much "épris" with Alix to be allowed to be much there without possibly ruining the happiness of all three.' Affie, she concluded, with growing terror, 'has not the strength of mind (or rather of principle and character) to resist the temptation and it is like playing with fire.' Queen Victoria had to rely on her conventional remedy: *he must marry early* lest he should 'again fall into sin from weakness'.

Victoria called on the dead Albert for reinforcements of repugnance against the indomitable sexuality of her healthy sons. Young Prince Leopold was ill again with the internal bleeding from haemophilia which occurred even after infinitesimal bruising from horse-riding. Yet the Queen weighed the distress of his fatal malady as nothing against the deplorable instincts of Edward and Alfred. 'Oh!' she lamented to Vicky in Berlin, 'the illness of a good child is so far less trying and distressing than the sinfulness of one's sons—like your two elder brothers. Oh! then one feels that death in purity is so far preferable to life in sin and degradation.'

But Edward staunchly maintained his rejection of the choice of death in purity.

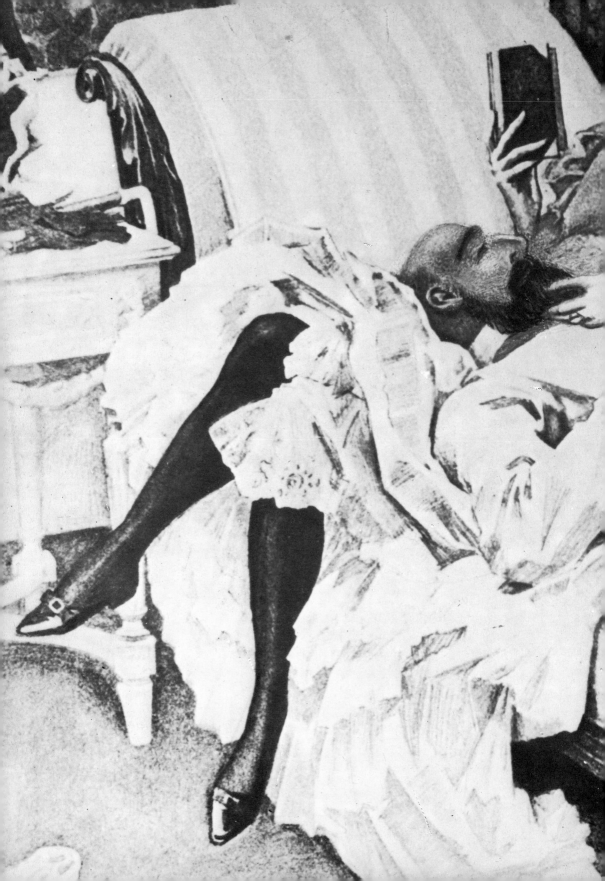

No Saint

Lord Carrington, the Prince's equerry and an officer in the Royal Horse Guards, was delighted to beg the participation of the newly married Prince and Princess of Wales in a ball given for the royal couple by the Household Brigade, the *corps d'élite* of ceremonial warriors whose special duty was to guard the persons of the Monarch and her family. The reception was carried out in high style, culminating in the arrival of the Prince and Princess. Then, as the band aired their instruments, two long files of Guards officers in full dress uniform strode into the ballroom. They drew their swords to shape a long arch, and down this shining cloister Edward and Alexandra danced in gaiety as they opened the ball. Queen Victoria snorted when she heard of it. Bertie and Alix were stretching the pace again.

Alexandra was oblivious of such censure, as yet cloudy and remote. She was eighteen, already the idol of her adopted nation, and living at last as a carefree princess in a Hans Christian Andersen world. She was pregnant, but scarcely aware of it. Babies were not the grim spoilers which they appeared to the Queen, but still part of the ethereal ecstasy. She certainly did not confide her condition to her mother-in-law. Queen Victoria was grumbling, 'Bertie goes on going out every night till she will become a skeleton, and hopes there cannot be.' The 'hopes' were of an heir, which Alexandra was already quietly carrying while she continued on what the Queen called 'one whirl of amusements . . . they are nothing but puppets running about for show all day and all night.'

The Queen could condemn, but the truth was she resolutely allowed her heir no other status but that of the chief social butterfly. She used him to the full as a layer of foundation stones, particularly if the edifice would eventually commemorate the dead Albert, but she refused to allow him to accept even the titular patronage of the learned societies, charitable institutions and social commissions which Albert had held, which had given him an influential role in the national establishment, and which was a part of the necessary royal performance. She directly forbade her Ministers to place the Prince of Wales 'in a position to which he is not entitled'.

Edward keenly resented this exclusion, yet very honourably avoided setting up any rival forum. His alternative Court was social, not political, whereas the classic role of the Hanoverian Princes of Wales in the eighteenth century had been to foment an alternative government, almost to head a formal Opposition.

On only one issue did Edward depart from this role. In early January 1864, almost casually, after a day spent sledging at Virginia

Water and watching Edward play ice-hockey, Alexandra gave birth to a two-months-premature son, christened Albert on the Queen's insistence and promptly called Eddy by everyone else. Almost immediately his parents were affected deeply by affairs of state. Just before the birth, Alexandra acknowledged the second crowned head in her immediate family. Her younger brother, aged seventeen, had already been nominated, chiefly through English influence, King of the Greeks. Now her father succeeded to the throne of Denmark. He was forced by popular demand to incorporate formally in his kingdom the disputed duchies of Schleswig

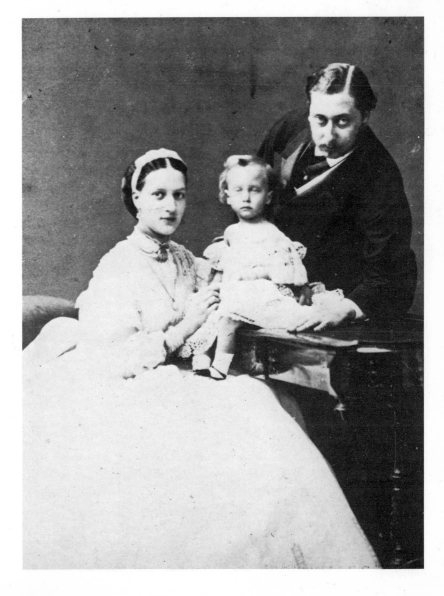

King Charles XV of Sweden introduced the Prince of Wales to a selection of Stockholm beauties when Edward wandered during Alexandra's second pregnancy.

and Holstein. Just after the birth, Prussian troops crossed the frontier and, supported by the Austrians, crushed the Danes. British political and public opinion wholeheartedly favoured the Danes. Queen Victoria was strongly pro-Prussian. The complicated dynastic issues did not really admit a black-and-white interpretation supporting either side, and in the event the British Government talked big and did nothing. Edward, not only because of Alexandra's understandable sentimental involvement, firmly supported the Danes, and lobbied the Conservative Opposition in order to intimidate the British Government into more positive action. He had the political sense to withdraw once the constitutional implications were emphasized to him, but his conception of the injustice of the final settlement did not waver, and he purposefully took his wife and baby on an informal visit to Denmark after the war was over.

Edward found Alexandra's family frankly boring, and escaped from Copenhagen to Stockholm, where the more worldly King Charles of Sweden introduced him to a selection of local beauties.

Alexandra was aware of her husband's activities, but so also, from the centre of her spider's web in Windsor, was Queen Victoria. The couple came home to receive a political roasting from Mama for their undiplomatic coolness to the Prussian Royal Family whom they had visited on the return journey—Alexandra unaffectedly hated the Prussians for life after 1864. But Victoria' gave her daughter-in-law more sympathetic support for the sexual tolerance that had now to be extended. 'Her lot is no easy one,' the Queen noted. 'But she is very fond of Bertie, though not blind.'

Thus, twenty months after the marriage, it was recognized that Edward had problems of fidelity. The immediate circumstances of the moment played their part in schooling Alexandra into an acceptance of this: she was pregnant with the baby who was to become King George V. But during the summer of that pregnancy a number of ladies, including a Dane, were noted as having created 'mischief' at Sandringham. The Duchess of Manchester was also on the scene, a gay, hard, gambling woman whom Queen Victoria consistently warned Edward and Alexandra against, as someone to be avoided for 'her *tone*, her love of admiration and *fast* style'. But Alexandra found the Duchess Louisa as socially fascinating as did her husband, even if the Princess's gentility and condition precluded her from joining Bertie and Louisa on some wild midnight dash by hansom cab to the music hall or the notorious riverside assignation-gardens at Cremorne.

Pregnancy barred Alexandra from the one pleasure-trip above all others that she longed for: the six-week stay in Russia for the wedding of her sister Dagmar to the Czarevitch Alexander. Edward went on her behalf, and reports filtered back of the scandalous attentions he paid to the ladies of Moscow and St Petersburg. On his return his behaviour towards his wife reached the peak of its unpleasantness. Five days before her confinement she developed an agonizing form of rheumatic fever which crippled her for six months and left her with a permanently damaged knee—the source of the 'Alexandra limp' which fashionable women copied as they did the Alexandra choker—and an acceleration of her hereditary deafness. Throughout this period of pain and tension Edward was almost brutally inconsiderate and self-centred.

The reason was that he had begun, and could not yet control, his lifelong infatuation with Paris, and a less permanent infatuation with an actress called Hortense Schneider.

The years of the 1860s covered the decade when 'gay' Paris was at its savagely extravagant peak, and Edward was already at home there. It was the age of the *grandes cocottes*, the fabled corps of courtesans who brought the Second Empire to its death-bed. There was Mamselle Maximum, so-called after the enormity of her fees, of her performance, of her clients, and of her extravagance. There was Cora Pearl, who could cozen £10,000 worth of diamonds from Prince Napoleon at one provocation, and who brought a banquet she gave for a score of gourmets to a triumphant climax by having herself served up on a silver salver carried by four footmen—Cora being naked and sprinkled with parsley. There was La Barucci, who proudly called herself 'the greatest whore in the world', and was presented as such to the young Prince of Wales. She had been briefed to behave properly and above all not to keep him waiting. She arrived at a private room in the Maison d'Or restaurant three-quarters of an hour late. 'Your Royal Highness,' said her sponsor, the Duke of Grammont-Caderousse, 'may I present the most unpunctual woman in France?' As La Barucci curtseyed, she dropped her clothes to the floor. The Duke reprimanded her. 'But you told me to be on my best behaviour to his Royal Highness,' she protested. 'I showed him the best I have, and it was free.'

There was also Hortense Schneider. She was not a prostitute, but she did have a soft heart. She was an actress who excelled in the operettas of Offenbach which were having their first productions in that decade. Besides the continuously revived *Orpheus in the Underworld,* Offenbach's ten productions in the 1860's included *La Vie Parisienne, Bluebeard,* and *La Belle Hélène,* in which Cora Pearl played Cupid, with not much on her torso but diamonds all over her boots. She even fell flat on her back at the end of the show to prove to the audience that there were diamonds set in the soles. Cora Pearl did it just for a lark, and went back to high-class whoring, but Hortense Schneider was a far more dedicated artist, a woman of wit and talent who created the main Offenbach roles and did much to create the Offenbach legend. The Marquis de Villemer said of her that she was 'exciting, modern, ironic—the froth of the champagne.' Such a description indicates the appeal and fascination she would have for a man with the tastes of the Prince of Wales.

La Schneider was not Edward's mistress on any long-term basis, no part of any Establishment as he later created it, with Lady Warwick, installed for seven years, and Mrs Alice Keppel, ruling for twelve, holding power for periods comparable with his own reign as King. Hortense was a generous woman who was flattered to receive Edward's attentions when he was in Paris or when she was in London. Yet she was not disposable merchandise. It is the fact that, lacking the extravagant abandon of the *grande cocotte,* she had a certain over-snobbish weakness for royalty—she exhibited

The marriage of Edward and Alexandra, *right*. 'You may think,' said Alexandra to Edward's sister Vicky just before the wedding ceremony, 'you may think that I like marrying Bertie for his position. But if he were a cowboy I would love him just the same and would marry no one else.' The bride and groom: Edward in Garter robes, Alexandra in a gown of silver tissue trimmed with Honiton lace.

Right, overleaf. Rival theatre programmes. Gertie Millar is portrayed in the Gaiety Theatre production of Lionel Monckton's musical *The Orchid*, set — in Edward's honour — in Nice on the Promenade des Anglais.

Right, second overleaf. Current picture postcard reaction to the Entente Cordiale, born most unexpectedly in May 1903. In a personal visit to Paris Edward converted the previously icy attitude of President Loubet and the French public, but infuriated the German Ambassador, seen dancing after him as his lackey. President Loubet paid a return visit to London via North Africa.

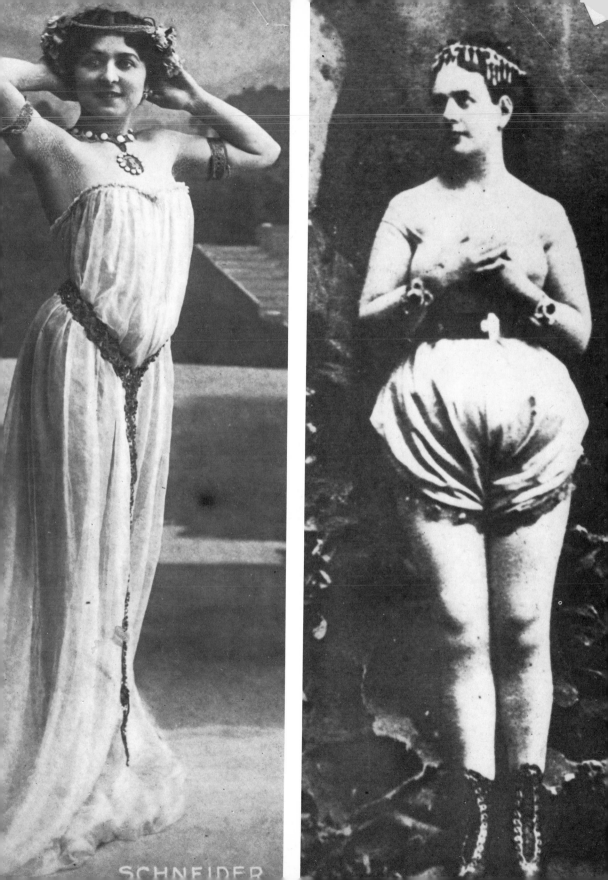

SCHNEIDER

this penchant so frequently later that she was called *'le passage des princes'.* But Edward never regarded her as bound exclusively to him, and he accepted with equanimity during his liaison with her that Lord Carrington, to whom he had relinquished Nellie Clifden, was Hortense's escort and companion through the feverish fortnight of the Baden-Baden summer race meeting.

The clue to Edward's courtship of Hortense Schneider, and to the whole mystique of the domination of the courtesans of the nineteenth century, lies in a Gallic approach to women, not yet imported into Great Britain. Vicky, Crown Princess of Prussia, once summed up French bawdry, by comparison with 'the coarseness of my beloved Shakespeare', by saying that, while Shakespeare 'gives the worst names to the worst things and makes every improper thing revolting, the French make improper things interesting and gloss wickedness over', which, she said, was a thousand times worse. But this gloss was highly acceptable to French masculine Society, and a part of their social intercourse which Edward joyfully accepted and welcomed.

Beauty itself was a commodity which demanded a certain conventional devotion. There was an admitted objective brutality mingled with the aesthetic admiration. Young men were brought up to appreciate a fine woman by matching her to a catalogue of classic points, as if she were a high-bred horse or a Ming vase. It was Napoleon III, long before Rudyard Kipling, who said that he enjoyed a woman as he might savour a good cigar after dinner. But at the same time there was a semi-religious cult of devotion to beauty.

Men literally paid court to courtesans. They were flattering in their devotion before they progressed to the commercial plane, and they were ingeniously thoughtful in the gifts they offered, even if the most influential present was still based on diamonds or a beautifully bound volume of bank-notes. This cult of beauty was transferred to late nineteenth-century Britain. Many of the professional 'beauties' who were celebrated in widely popular picture postcards were basically prostitutes. But there was still a more-than-formal devotion to their beauty, and men were proud and boastful when they were accepted by these women, even when the world knew that a stiff price had been paid.

Hortense Schneider was the first of Edward's mistresses whose name was publicly printed in British journals, even in *The Times*, often in execration of the Prince's licentious habits, but still with an aura of rueful envy of the sport that was going on. This publicity, which began in 1867, when Edward was being most obviously

Hortense Schneider, *above and left overleaf,* applied herself so assiduously to acting as mistress to royalties that she became known as *le passage des princes.* Her rival, Caroline Letessier, said of her I've never seen an uglier cow.' Schneider created the rôles of many Offenbach heroines and set his charm. She was the first of Edward's mistresses to be publicly named in the Press.

One of the gay lights of Edward's Paris, Cora Pearl gave a banquet at which she was served naked on a silver salver... sprinkled with parsley.

neglectful of the sick Alexandra, marked a change in the attitude towards the British Royal Family, which had been given markedly circumspect treatment since 1840. It heralded a new freedom of criticism.

This outspokenness did not stop at reflections on the Prince of Wales. The Queen herself was not untouched. The nation was tired of the years of ostentatious seclusion indulged in by the mourning Widow. Historians who concentrate their attention on the 'bad press' accorded to the Prince of Wales give insufficient weight to the signs of a deeper dissatisfaction with the Queen. There was a considerable body of opinion as early as 1868 which campaigned for her abdication. Consequently a delicate balance had to be maintained in any denigration of the Prince of Wales, for he would be her successor, if only as regent. Republicanism became stronger ten years later, but for the moment the desired revolution was seen as changing the sovereign, not eradicating the monarchy.

This ambivalence was especially marked in the satirical magazine *Tomahawk* which ran for three years from 1867. Tomahawk was a man—no Red Indian, but Arthur à Beckett, son of one of the original staff of *Punch*. He announced himself: 'My name is Tomahawk and I wield a hatchet with a very sharp edge. . . . Regardless of the taunts of fools, liars, or snobs Tomahawk will continue to use his hatchet as a weapon for the protection of the weak.'

When the hatchet was applied to etch a political cartoon, its force and subtlety were superior to the productions of *Punch* at that time. The text was often more laboured; pointed but schoolboyish. In *Tomahawk's* second number he printed a burlesque speech supposed to have been delivered by the Prince of Wales at the laying of the foundation stone of the Albert Hall of Arts and Sciences:

> This is to be the Hall of Arts and Sciences. My royal mother is going to lay the foundation stone. I wish she would perform her duty to the living as well as she does her duty to the dead. I think Knowles[1] writes me shocking bad speeches. . . . I don't know what this place is to be, I believe a sort of west-end music hall. I've been obliged to take a private box. . . . I suppose I must say something about this stupid place. It has been got up by puffing and gentle pressure. Lots of fellows have taken boxes, because they were afraid of offending my mother. They wish they had not done it. . . . If we say it's all in memory of my father, Parliament will be obliged to vote the money. . . . I always say in my speeches that I want to walk in my father's footsteps, but I don't. I think you may praise a man too much, even when he's dead.

1 ie Knollys. General Sir William Knollys was the Prince's Comptroller and Treasurer; his son Sir Francis, later Lord Knollys, became Private Secretary.

It makes people tired of him. I believe that hideous conglomeration of bricks and cranes opposite [ie the Albert Memorial] is a memorial to him. I thought it had something to do with the Main Drainage Works. The nation has to pay for it, and did not like it. I don't think they'll pay for another. . . . I shan't say any more. The public thinks the whole affair is a bore, and so do I.

A few weeks later the Schneider affair was receiving calculated publicity, along with an attack on the degradation of the London theatres—'haunts of semi-nudity and disgusting double entendres, now patronized almost exclusively by profligates'. Edward was not moved by such condemnation. When the can-can was introduced into the Lyceum and the Alhambra—the diversion, adopted by Offenbach, is even to this day described in the *Oxford English Dictionary* as 'a dance performed at the public halls of Paris with extravagant and indecent gestures'—Edward took Alexandra along to enjoy it, and gave a new seal of approval to the lighter London theatre.

Tomahawk printed a cartoon which exploited one of the two parallels that were applied *ad nauseam* to Edward at this time: the identification with George Prince of Wales, the Regent Rake, later George IV, who debased the metal of the British monarchy to such a degree that living memories still shuddered; and the identification with a semi-fictional Prince of Wales, Shakespeare's creation of the Prince Hal who fooled with Falstaff, tore a sheet with bawdy Doll, and profaned the Lord Chief Justice, all on the rather prim understanding with the audience that there would be an endearing reformation and a pure King Henry V soon:

> When this loose behaviour I throw off
> And pay the debt I never promisèd.

The theme selected on this occasion was that of the Prince Regent. The setting of the cartoon was on the battlements of Elsinore. The Ghost of Hamlet's father beckoned to the son, who shook off the restraining arms of his companions and strained after the apparition. But the Ghost had the features of Prinny and Hamlet's appearance was as Edward. The caption read: 'The Prince of Wales to King George IV, *"I'll follow thee!"* '

A few weeks later the artist, Matt Morgan, produced his most famous cartoon, this time directed at the alleged domination of Queen Victoria and the nation by her unpopular 'Highland Servant', John Brown. It showed an empty throne, a crown under a glass case, and a masterful Highlander contemptuously turning his back on both. It was entitled 'A Brown Study.' Over the following month *The Times* discussed abdication as the solution to the

Queen's neglect of her essential public duties, and *Tomahawk* strongly urged that the Prince of Wales should be appointed Regent:

> If three weeks is the longest period which the Sovereign is able to spend in the Imperial capital during each year, if all the functions which the Head of the Realm should discharge have to be vicariously discharged by the Heir Apparent and his Consort, it is evidently for the true interest and well-being of the Queen, as well as of the nation, that a Regency Bill should be passed as soon as possible. Six years [the length of the Queen's mourning] is a long probation, and if, that probation having been passed, the energies of the Queen are still so overwhelmed by her great sorrow to affect materially the discharge of her important duties, it is surely far more considerate towards both the Sovereign and the woman that she should be relieved from the distressing weight which the unavoidable neglect of such duties must occasion to her sensitive and conscientious nature.

> . . . There is nothing unconstitutional in the establishment of a Regency. The Prince of Wales, whatever his faults, has ever shown himself most zealous and courteous in the performance of all his duties necessitated by his anomalous position. He has never attached himself to any political party. . . . He has travelled much, and has divested himself of those insular prejudices which characterize some Englishmen, while on all material points his sympathies are with all that is good in the British temperament. He is certainly not a petty German despot either by nature or by education. His filial affection is undoubted; his promotion to the Regency could occasion no private or

Edward Prince of Wales, as Hamlet, sees the Ghost of George the Prince Regent, and swears 'I'll follow thee' — which was a constant fear of his mother Victoria, terror-stricken by the thought of any hereditary traits being transmitted from her 'wicked uncle'.

public jealousy; in fact it is difficult to conceive any Prince who could be so unobjectionable a candidate for such a difficult position.

The urgency of this campaign rose toa note of desperation when it was realized that Edward and Alexandra had committed themselves to leave England for six months during the winter and spring of 1868-9. 'Let Majesty come forth now,' cried Tomahawk in an appeal to the Queen; 'surely, could the dead speak, he for whom you mourn would solemnly adjure you to do that which is your duty . . . not wait till those who hate monarchy ask with ruthless persistence: "Where is the Sovereign, the paid servant of the State? Why should we vote annually a sum for certain purposes which are still every year unfulfilled?" ' And the cartoonist produced a dramatic plea to the Prince of Wales entitled 'Don't Desert Me', showing Britannia on her knees and the British Lion weeping as the Prince prepared to sail away.

Edward and Alexandra were going away to try and reach a new understanding. They were going away from the public innuendoes against the Prince's amorous inclinations which had become more persistent during yet another pregnancy of his wife. The name of Hortense Schneider was now a common sneer. Edward demonstrated his cool nerve by going to Paris and urbanely taking Alexandra to see Schneider in the theatre. They then travelled on a gay route by way of Copenhagen, Berlin, Vienna, and Trieste, to board

'Don't Desert Me!' Part of the strong Press build-up against Edward's visit to Egypt at a time when Victoria was taking no part in national life.

the frigate *Ariadne* for a visit to Egypt. The Prince took thirty-three servants but included no women in his party, save a lady waiting upon Princess Alexandra. He did, however, include in his suite Lord Carrington and the Honourable Oliver Montagu, second son of the Earl of Sandwich, another officer in the Royal Horse Guards.

At Alexandria they were joined by a crony of the Prince, vehemently disapproved of by the Queen. This was the Duke of Sutherland, and, apart from women, the principal passions which he shared with Edward were to drive fire engines (horse-drawn) and to drive railway engines (steam-propelled), both very fast. Their close friend was Captain Eyre Shaw, who virtually created the London Fire Brigade, and earned a more lasting accolade from Gilbert:

> Oh, Captain Shaw!
> Type of true love kept under,
> Could thy Brigade
> With cold cascade
> Quench my great love, I wonder!

Edward's friendship with Shaw highlights an important facet of his personality. He was generous with the honours he sponsored or bestowed, and by imaginative selection and an absence of stuffiness in his own choice of friends he extended the nation's recognition to areas where honours had been previously thought incongruous. Through his influence knighthoods were awarded not only to the first Fire Chief, Shaw, but to the first actor, Henry Irving, who declined at first and accepted twelve years later, and the first journalist, W. H. 'Billy' Russell, 'Russell of *The Times*,' the war correspondent and foreign reporter, who was a member of Sutherland's party for the Nile trip.

The Duke of Sutherland had four other guests, the necessary additional domestic servants, and Alister the piper, without whom he never travelled. Together they steamed up the Nile in a convoy of blue-and-gold boats and floating kitchens. One lighter in tow carried horses and a riding-donkey for the Princess. A store-boat had a cargo of 3000 bottles of champagne, 20,000 of soda-water and 4000 bottles of claret, 'with sherry, ale and liqueurs'—no miserly supply for a group of twenty tourists on a six-weeks river jaunt. Supported by the strains of the bagpipes they had a memorably beefy time, cursorily inspecting a few antiquities but always with a weather eye open for game, for they shot everything which moved, from crocodile to quail.

Alexandra conceived another child. They came home by way of Constantinople, the Crimea, Athens and Corfu, and managed a final six-day run-down in Paris. They reached London on 12 May, went straight to the Royal Academy to open the London season, and attended a Court Concert that night. 'There is no rest for the wicked,' observed Edward resiliently, but the unfortunate accompaniment was that there was also no comfort for the Princess of Wales through her pregnancy. Even in Egypt the couple had heard the preliminary thunder of an incipient Society scandal, and it rumbled menacingly throughout the year. The storm broke after Alexandra had borne her fifth child, being then twenty-four years old. Sir Charles Mordaunt sued his wife Harriett for divorce on the grounds of adultery with Viscount Cole and Sir Frederick Johnstone on stated dates, and with 'other persons' between 15 June 1868 and 28 February 1869. Amongst those other persons, it was well understood, Sir Charles Mordaunt included the Prince of Wales, and Edward was served with a subpoena to attend court as a witness in the case.

The Mordaunt Case was a divorce trial with a curious defence. Counsel for Lady Mordaunt claimed that, though she had admitted adultery with Lord Cole, Sir Frederick Johnstone and the Prince of Wales, and although Sir Charles Mordaunt produced circumstantial details against them, she had been insane at the time of her confession, was still insane at the time of the trial, and was therefore unfit to plead. If the jury decided that the respondent was insane, Sir Charles Mordaunt had no case. Yet all the 'bedroom evidence' and the usual depositions from hotel chambermaids were presented in full. Against this, Counsel for Lady Mordaunt called the Prince of Wales, alone of the three alleged adulterers, as a witness for the defence. It was a tortuous and tenuous logic: why not call Cole and Johnstone, against whom adultery on specific dates and in specific places was alleged? But it at least gave the Prince the opportunity to deny in public any charge against him. Neither the Prince of Wales, nor the Queen, nor the troubled British Government conceived the slightest enthusiasm for this chance to 'wash dirty linen in public', even if the underwear could be declared to have been clean all the time. But the Prince was advised not to claim privilege, but to obey the witness summons. The Lord Chancellor, however, gave private assurances to the Queen that the judge, Lord Penzance, would protect the Prince against improper questions.

The case lasted ten days, and, characteristically, the Prince decided to attend every sitting of the court, rather than appear at a convenient time by private arrangement. Unfortunately Lord Penzance did make some adjustments to the sittings, and give the Prince the freedom of his private room. For this he was duly

Sir Eyre Massey Shaw, W. S. Gilbert's Captain Shaw, Chief of the Metropolitan Fire Brigade, was an adventurous intimate of Edward's and took him to all the best fires.

The Prince and Princess of Wales among their suite on the Egyptian tour. Sitting on the steps, right, is the explorer Sir Samuel Baker.

The blue-and-gold dahabieh which accommodated Edward and Alexandra on their trip up the Nile. An accompanying store-boat carried 30,000 bottles of liquid refreshment.

lambasted by the Press, which alleged over-solicitude for 'the Royal Breakfast, the Most Gracious Cigar, the Matutinal Siesta'. It was a *cause célèbre* which fired every spark of reaction against privilege.

Lady Mordaunt had been a friend of the Prince before her marriage in 1866, at the age of seventeen. She met the Princess later. Sir Charles Mordaunt, who had been the Member of Parliament for South Warwickshire, was considerably older than his wife and, after his marriage, continued his bachelor habit of going alone on fishing trips to Norway. The Prince of Wales had often called on Lady Mordaunt in London, and Sir Charles and Lady Mordaunt had attended a ball at Abergeldie, the Scottish house of the Prince and Princess of Wales near Balmoral. Lady Mordaunt was then some months pregnant, and her baby was born in the early spring of 1869.

The baby was born virtually blind. Harriett Mordaunt was greatly affected by this, and any normal puerperal depression was deepened. Rightly or wrongly, she concluded that the baby's condition was caused by venereal disease which she had caught from another man. She then made the confession to her husband on which his case rested.

Sir Charles Mordaunt, giving evidence in chief under the examination of his Counsel, said,

> I was aware that the Prince of Wales had an acquaintance with my wife. I had spoken to his Royal Highness but was never intimate with him. I was aware that he was on visiting terms with her family. He never came to my house at my invitation. I warned my wife against continuing the acquaintance with his Royal Highness for reasons which governed my own mind.
>
> I told her that I had heard in various quarters certain circumstances connected with the Prince's character which caused me to make that remark. I did not enter into particulars. At that time I had seen the Prince once at my house. I was not aware till after my wife's confinement that the Prince had been a constant visitor at my house, and that any correspondence existed between them.

Sir Charles said that he again asked Lady Mordaunt not to continue to receive the Prince of Wales. This occurred when he had come home early from shooting one day. No visitor was in the house, but after he had gone to lie down for a rest he was told that the Prince of Wales had called. He went down and saw him, and later told his wife not to receive the Prince again.

He then went on to relate a conversation about Sir Frederick Johnstone which his wife had prompted. She was pregnant at the time. She asked him why Sir Frederick Johnstone had never mar-

Sir Charles Mordaunt
found letters from the
Prince of Wales inside a
locked desk of his wife's.
'I have done very wrong
with the Prince of Wales,'
she told him. 'Often, and
in open day.'

ried. Sir Charles replied that he understood that Johnstone had
never married 'because he had had a disease, several times'.

After the baby was born, with what was clearly a serious condition of the eyes, Lady Mordaunt said to her husband, on the third
day, 'Charlie, I have deceived you. You are not the father of that
child.' Mordaunt said he made no reply at all There was a long
pause. Finally, he stated, Lady Mordaunt said, 'Lord Cole is the
father of it, and I am the cause of its blindness.'

Mordaunt said that there was then a silence lasting a quarter of an hour. His wife then burst into tears. She said, 'Charlie, I have been very wicked. I have done very wrong.'

'Who with?' asked Mordaunt.

His wife's reply was: 'With Lord Cole, Sir Frederick Johnstone, the Prince of Wales, and others, often, and in open day.'[1]

Sir Charles did not attest that he made any reply to his wife's outburst. But he said he got possession of a key to his wife's locked desk and opened it. He found there a number of letters from the Prince of Wales, with some dried flowers and the verses of a valentine. There was also a handkerchief of the Prince of Wales's loose in the desk.

The 'Mordaunt letters' which the Prince sent to Harriett, and she too piously kept, are always glossed over by Edward's apologists as 'indiscreet, but trifling', and immediately ignored. They are never printed. The major wrong done by this omission has been to the character of King Edward the Seventh himself. Whether he did or did not make love with Harriett Mordaunt is of passing importance. What the letters show is that he did not seduce her. She was chasing him, and he, for most of the time, was more long-suffering than ardent. But there must always come a time when Cerberus takes the sop.

The first of the dozen letters from the Prince of Wales ran:

Sandringham, January 13, 1867

My dear Lady Mordaunt,
   I am quite shocked never to have answered your kind letter—written some time ago—nor to have thanked you for the very pretty muffetees [knitted extra cuffs, or mittens] which are very useful this cold weather. I had no idea where you had been staying since your marriage. . . . I hope to have the pleasure of seeing you and making the acquaintance of Sir Charles.

Ever yours most sincerely,
Albert Edward.

The next letter, written five weeks later at the beginning of Alexandra's long bout of rheumatic fever, gave the news that she had given birth to their daughter Louise, and continued: 'I hope you will come to the Oswald and St James's Hall this week. There would, I am sure, be no harm your remaining till Saturday in town. I shall like to see you again.'

1 'Open day' was, to the public mind, the shocking, even damning, phrase because daylight intercourse, which in later years it was conceded that the Prince of Wales had introduced into social etiquette, was still unacceptably unconventional.

108

A letter of May 1867 thanked Lady Mordaunt for sending a ladies' umbrella which she had brought from Paris and asked if there were any commission he could do for her in return since he was going to Paris next week (to see Hortense Schneider).

A letter dated October 1867 acknowledged photographs, and went on:

> We are all delighted with Hamilton's marriage, and I think you are rather hard on the young lady, as, although not exactly pretty, she is very popular with everyone. From his letter he seems to be very much in love—a rare occurrence now-a-days. . . . I saw in the papers that you were in London on Saturday. I wish you had let me know, as I would have made a point of calling. There are some good plays going on, and we are going the rounds of them.

Two letters in November 1867 referred to some of the Prince's ponies which Lady Mordaunt was insisting on buying. The second of them, written from Sandringham, said that Oliver and Blandford (the Honourable Oliver Montagu and the Marquess of Blandford, heir to the Duke of Marlborough) had given up the idea of creating hell in Algiers in favour of bringing it to Sandringham: 'Oliver has been in great force, and as bumptious as ever. Blandford is also here, so you can imagine what a row goes on.' This is an interesting sidelight on the character of Oliver Montagu, later the Prince's equerry and Colonel of the Blues (the Royal Horse Guards), who has become famous for the idealistic love affair which he maintained with Princess Alexandra for twenty-six years until he died, unmarried, in 1893. Whenever Montagu was present at a reception it was he, not Edward, who always danced the first after-supper waltz with Alexandra. Alexandra's official biographer, Georgina Battiscombe, says, 'There is no doubt that Oliver Montagu loved her . . . but equally there is no doubt that he was not her lover.' Edward's last official biographer, Sir Philip Magnus, asserts, 'He loved the Princess with that exalted, chivalrous and selfless passion which inspired knights in mediaeval romances to dedicate their lives to the service of beautiful princesses and queens. Oliver Montagu would have perished gladly to spare the Princess of Wales the least shadow of reproach or annoyance.' It adds depth to the portrait to know that he was also the hearty sporting extrovert who with his crony Blandford could turn Sandringham into a bear garden, and he had a considerable youthful reputation as a womanizer. In a note which Edward sent to Lord Carrington in Paris at about this time asking Carrington to pick up the Prince's horse-racing winnings in Carrington's name, Edward asked, 'Remember

Colonel the Hon. Oliver Montagu, commanding the Blues (Royal Horse Guards), was equerry to the Prince of Wales and the chaste lover of Alexandra, who returned the same affection *sans reproche.*

me to those wicked boys Blandford and Oliver.' As a wicked boy, the Marquess of Blandford was to involve the Prince of Wales in the next scandal in line after the Mordaunt divorce affair.

Other notes from the Prince to Lady Mordaunt referred to Sir Frederick Johnstone, who was staying at Sandringham but going on to stay with the Mordaunts for the Warwick race-meeting. Finally, on the eve of his six-months absence in Europe and Egypt, Edward wrote: 'I shall not see you for a long time, but trust to find you perhaps in London on our return. If you should have time, it will be very kind of you to write me sometimes.'

In Lord Penzance's court there was a week of the usual tangled and insinuating evidence usual in a divorce case. Lady Mordaunt's servants had to give evidence about the times people came out of her bedroom. Her maid was required to testify that when the Prince of Wales visited Lady Mordaunt alone he usually stayed from four o'clock to five-thirty or six, and did not come in a private carriage. The Prince of Wales was then called into the witness box.

Lord Penzance first said:

It is my duty to point out to his Royal Highness his position under the Act of Parliament passed last session. It provides that no witness in any proceeding, whether a party to the suit or not, shall be liable to be asked, or be bound to answer, any questions tending to show that he or she has been guilty of adultery. Now, from the course which the case has taken, I think it right to point this out to his Royal Highness, and to tell him that he is not bound or required by law to submit to any interrogations on that subject.

Counsel for Lady Mordaunt then began to take the Prince through a carefully charted testimony.

'I believe your Royal Highness has for some time been acquainted with the Mordaunt family?'

'I have.'

'Were you acquainted with Lady Mordaunt before her marriage?'

'I was.'

'On her marriage did your Royal Highness write to her and make her some wedding present?'

'I did.'

'Previous to her marriage had she visited at Marlborough House when your Royal Highness and the Princess of Wales were there?'

'She has.'

'And has she gone to the theatre with both your Royal Highnesses?'

'She has.'

'We are told that she was married at the end of 1866. In 1867 did you see much of her?'

'I did.'

'And in the year 1868?'

'I did also.'

'Were you acquainted with Sir Charles Mordaunt?'
'I was.'
'Have you frequently met him?'
'I have.'
'And with Lady Mordaunt?'
'With Lady Mordaunt.'

Counsel then went into irritatingly precise detail to show that Sir Charles Mordaunt was better acquainted with the Prince of Wales than he had claimed, and that both had participated in a pigeon-shooting match at Hurlingham at which Lady Mordaunt was present and the Prince of Wales 'spoke to Lady Mordaunt when Sir Charles was by'.

Counsel said, 'We have heard in the course of this case that your Royal Highness uses hansom cabs occasionally. I do not know whether it is so?'

'It is so,' said the Prince. Counsel had now established, he hoped, that if the Prince arrived at Lady Mordaunt's house by cab it was not so that his private carriage should not be recognized as it waited, but was a fairly usual occurrence.

Counsel then said, 'I have only one more question to trouble your Royal Highness with. Has there ever been improper familiarity or criminal act between yourself and Lady Mordaunt?'

In a very firm tone the Prince declared, 'There has not', and a burst of applause spluttered through the Court. It was promptly quelled. Sir Charles's Counsel said he would not cross-examine, and the Prince left the box to further stifled applause.

The judge had plainly said that the Prince was not liable to be asked, or bound to answer, any interrogation on his alleged adultery. The question had, nevertheless, been put and answered. Sir Frederick Johnstone promptly intervened through his advocate to ask if he, as a named co-respondent, could also deny adultery. This was allowed, and he duly denied adultery. But he also wanted to add to the debate on Sir Charles Mordaunt's opinion that he had never married because he had had a venereal disease several times. His Counsel accordingly gave him this opportunity, and framed the question for him.

Johnstone said, 'A more unfounded statement was never made behind a man's back. It is perfectly untrue.'

But he was cross-examined. And opposing Counsel slyly asked, 'You do not mean to imply that you have never suffered?'

'Certainly not,' conceded Sir Frederick Johnstone. 'I have had youthful indiscretions.'

It is an interesting aspect of the social values of the time that he exposed himself to such a question, and was content to stand on a record of confining his syphilis to his youth. To modern ears it has the unrealistic ring of the housemaid's answer when she was forced to admit to her mistress that she had had an illegitimate baby. 'But it was only a little one, ma'am.'

After ten days of trial, the judge summed up. He told the jury, 'It must be a matter of congratulation to you that, as a result of what can be proved, the advocate for Sir Charles honestly and fairly says: "This is all I can put before you to justify the statements which Lady Mordaunt made shortly after her confinement in relation to the Prince, and I do not now impute that he was guilty of the crime of adultery." '

After retiring for only ten minutes the jury found that Lady Mordaunt was, through insanity, unfit to plead. Sir Charles Mordaunt had lost his case.[1] It had been avidly followed by the general public, and the Prince of Wales was solidly unpopular. Alexandra, understandably shaken and depressed by the whole incident, had the nation's sympathy. But it was no consolation to her to be wildly cheered when she entered a box in a theatre, and to hear the cheers change to hisses, boos and catcalls when her husband followed her.

The Prince of Wales was virulently attacked in the press for months after the Mordaunt affair. *Tomahawk* protested that the campaign had gone too far, and, in fact, the *Sheffield Daily Telegraph* was successfully sued for libel over comments it had printed. *Tomahawk* wrote:

We have no wish to paint Albert Edward Prince of Wales as a saint. There seems no chance of Pio Nono [*Pope Pius IX*] canonizing the Heir Apparent just at present. His Royal Highness is a cultivated Englishman, and (if we may be permitted to say, without impropriety) a very good fellow. He seriously has a great deal to do, and he does that great deal well. The Nation should be lenient with him. The number of foundation-stones he has to lay, and after-dinner speeches he has to listen to, must be something enormous. Men about town 'in retreat' will tell you that of all the dreadful bores upon earth, the greatest and most dreadful is 'Society'. Now the Prince sees the very worst side of Society.

But, in its previous issue, even *Tomahawk* had not been able to resist a snide juvenile witticism: 'It has recently been the fashion to libel, and cruelly to libel, the Heir Apparent to our Throne. Why, we know not, unless it is that everything connected with W(h)ales must be *fishy!*'

1 Five years later he did win another divorce case, naming only Lord Cole as co-respondent.

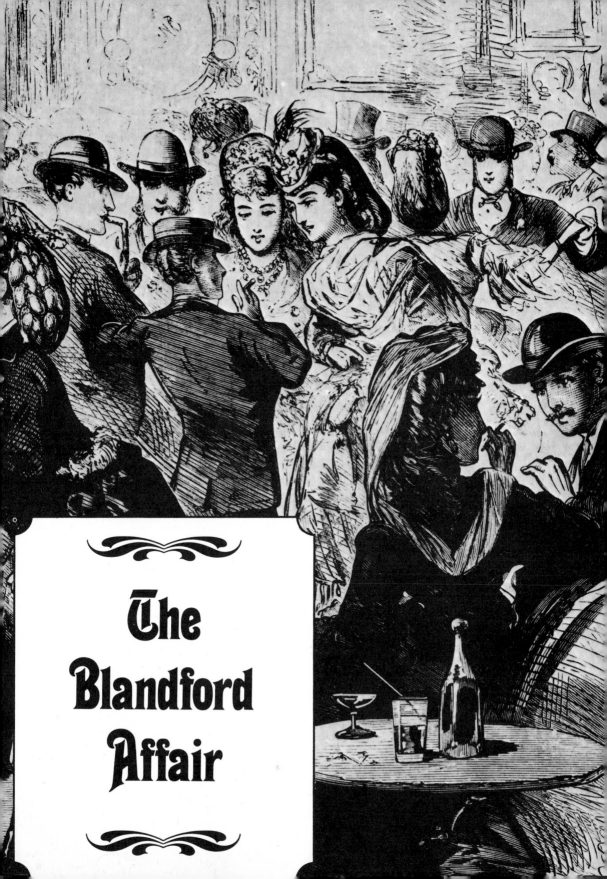

The Blandford Affair

I T had been socially and constitutionally dangerous for the Prince of Wales to appear in the Divorce Court. The secrets of the upper class could be kept only if they were successfully excluded from the national press, but a divorce case was a public action. Its details could not then, by law, be kept out of the press, and consequently were splashed all over the press of every cultural level, as the only legalized, circulation-raising pornography. A divorce case within the ruling class was therefore a sign of social failure, by breach of the unwritten rule that knowledge of upper-class scandals should be limited to upper-class people or their confidants.

With republicanism becoming more popular, any stick in the 1870s was good enough to beat British royalty. If an editor wished to assert that the Prince of Wales had been seen incapably drunk on the Boulevard des Italiens, he printed it, implausible though that situation was to anyone who knew the Prince. When a baby was born to one of Victoria's children—a fairly frequent occurrence during this decade—*Reynolds's Newspaper* could dive to extremities of coarseness in advocating strict birth control for the Royal Family

> Our Royal family is prodigiously prolific. . . . The Royal incubation of princes and princesses is to be deplored. . . . A special race is springing up amongst us with a rapidity that excites astonishment, who will consider itself privileged to live without labour, to waste their lives in luxury, idleness, frivolity, and, may be, vice, and to do this at the nation's cost. They should exercise restraint, curb indulgence, and not allow the Royal breed to develop into a mere litter.

The Prince of Wales was, however, purged of much of his unpopularity by falling dangerously ill with typhoid fever in late 1871, and the nation ironically woke up to the fact that he was, after all, still the 'very good fellow' they had once declared him. One publication gave him a new motto for his crest, *Enim ille est dexter bonus socius* (dog-Latin for 'For he's a right good fellow'). During the delirium at the height of his fever Alexandra had to be kept out of his bedroom because he was being too frank about his escapades and naming too many names in his ravings. As soon as he became conscious again he called for a bottle of Bass's ale. In the springtime there was a national thanksgiving service at St Paul's Cathedral which did much for the popularity of the Royal Family, since not only the Prince and his popular Princess, but also Queen Victoria, who had not attended such a public function for ten years, submitted to the cheering. No gratitude to Providence, however, could be permitted to alter Edward's formula for attendance at ordinary Sunday church service at Sandringham. He habitually ordered a ten-minute sermon, and even then waited until the service was half over before he made his entry, to a special peal of bells.

Edward confirmed his return to good health by breaking into the gossip sheets on the strength of a few larks with brother Affie, Duke of Edinburgh. What the papers did not know was that he and his brother were so resolute in the pursuit of actresses at that time that they asked Lord Rosebery, then an up-and-coming twenty-six-year-old politician, later Liberal Prime Minister, to grant them the use of his London house as a place of assignation. For more strictly conventional gentlemanly pursuits, Edward had by this time founded the Marlborough Club, opposite Marlborough House at 52 Pall Mall. It had been started in a huff when Edward found that smoking cigars in White's was severely restricted, and he instituted the rule in the Marlborough that smoking was allowed everywhere except in the dining-room. Edward also founded the New Club at Evan's Music Hall in Covent Garden, a late-night haunt where, as an instance of his remarkable tolerance of minorities such as the Catholics and the Jews, the rousing choruses were led by a singing

To Evans's Music Hall in Covent Garden Edward used to drive for regular midnight performances from the time of his twenties. Later he founded the New Club at Evans's, where the somewhat rowdy choruses were sung by Catholic choirmen from St George's Cathedral, Southwark.

company recruited from choristers at St George's Southwark, then the Catholic Cathedral of Westminster: but the airs were not principally pious. To Evans's at midnight the carriages rolled up with Edward's prime cronies: beefy Lord Alfred Paget, the Earl of Aylesford, and Lord Dupplin, all betting on whether they would hear that night the rival, but equally popular band of the Blue or the Red Hungarians.

Soon the Duke of Edinburgh safely escaped his fixation on London actresses, with which the Press was now openly taunting him, by marrying the daughter of the Czar of Russia. Edward and Alexandra went to the wedding, and came back to England to plan the most ostentatious social function of their long career.

It was a fancy dress ball in Marlborough House. Alexandra went as a Venetian lady (wearing a Juliet cap, which was Veronese), with her two young sons, Prince Eddy and Prince George as her pages. Edward dressed as King Charles I, with a blonde Cavalier wig and a cascade of diamonds branching from his hat. Edward did not object to fancy dress: his obsession with uniforms may be cited in support of that. Above all, he indulged in the kilt, which was odd in the light of his mother's verdict that he was knock-kneed. The kilt was the garb of the Stuart kings, rather than the Hanoverians who had supplanted them. But it had been adopted with somewhat ludicrous gravity by the methodically romantic Albert of Saxe-Coburg when he and Victoria first acquired Balmoral, and both Victoria and Edward put their children into the kilt at the slightest ceremonial excuse, such as costume for a wedding. Even Kaiser Wilhelm of Germany inherited the addiction.

Edward, as he grew older, became a little more circumspect. If he went to Scotland by yacht he would adapt his costume day by day to the growing northern influence by instructing his valet every morning to put put 'something a little more Scottish' for him to wear, progressing through tweed to tartan until he could spring ashore in the kilt. Edward was aware of the incongruous effect that the skirt imposed on some Sassenachs and Germans who were required to adopt it in the Highlands. His letters to Lady Mordaunt included comments on the manner in which some of their mutual friends in London Society displayed themselves in the kilt. Even at Marlborough House in the heart of London, the first apparition confronting a visitor was a ghillie in the kilt, who, after a dour security glower, passed him on to two scarlet-coated and powdered footmen. It was, perhaps, Edward's answer to his mother's addiction to John Brown, whom the Prince cordially hated and who had even dominated the cavalcade to St Paul's Cathedral, sitting on the

The Princesse de Sagan, intermittently one of the more dependable French mistresses sought by Edward, presides over a costume ball at her château.

box of the Queen's carriage, 'very handsome in his full dress', as the doting Victoria saw him.

From the fancy dress ball, the Prince of Wales went without Alexandra to the love-nests and Casino of Baden, from which stately pleasure-dome his total gambling debts were quite erroneously reported to be £600,000. His next stop was Paris, which his Treasurer, General Sir William Knollys, described to the Queen as 'the most dangerous place in Europe, and it would be well if it was never re-visited'. Possibly the elderly General was galled by the fact that his son Francis, who was at that time as lusty as the Prince, was accompanying Edward while the father stayed at home. From Paris Edward started a private tour of the Loire Valley chateaux. These fastnesses were then occupied by pugnacious representatives of the French aristocracy who were, in the male line, resolutely bloody-minded at their loss of status in the new Third Republic and, in the female line, often amorously attached to the Prince of Wales.

One of their leaders, the Princesse Jeanne de Sagan, had been intimately acquainted with Edward since before his marriage. She was only spasmodically reconciled with her husband, who was conceded to be as lecherous as she, but rather wittier. On one of

The most spectacular fancy-dress function which Edward ever attended was the Historical Costume Ball given at Devonshire House in July 1897 by the Double Duchess' — Louisa, former Duchess of Manchester, translated to be Duchess of Devonshire after Lord 'Harty-Tarty' Hartington had succeeded to his father's dukedom and made an honest woman of the mistress whose long liaison even Queen Victoria had to condone in her Minister.

Edward Prince of Wales went as the Grand Master of the Knights Hospitallers of Malta.

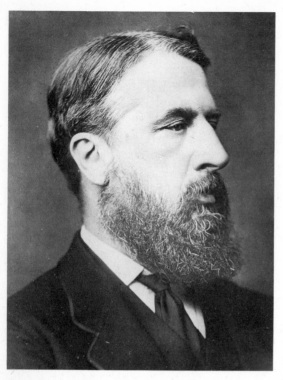

these rare reunions, in 1867, she bore her second son after a minimum of re-cohabitation with her spouse, whom she had not favoured with her company for nine years. Inevitably the Paris gossips speculated whether her reconciliation after so long a separation had anything to do with a sojourn with the Prince of Wales two months previously. She was remembered for having delivered herself of one *bon mot:* 'A husband can hope to be a hero in his wife's eyes only for two months—the month before he is married and the month after his death.' The Princesse de Sagan evidently brought up her children to express themselves just as pungently and even more practically. On the occasion of this particular visit, in 1874, of Edward to her castle of Mello, her elder son came into his mother's boudoir during the afternoon. He saw a man's clothing on a sofa. In a rage, he seized the clothes, ran out into the castle courtyard, and threw them in the fountain. The Prince of Wales emerged from the bedroom and was compelled to complain that he had nothing to wear. Since his girth was greater than any other gentleman within the household, and he had not brought a spare kilt, he was forced to leave the castle wearing extremely tight borrowed trousers.

Edward returned to London, was reunited with Alexandra, and

Lord Hartington, 'Harty-Tarty', later 8th Duke of Devonshire, a statesman whose liaison with the Duchess of Manchester had to be grudgingly accepted even by Queen Victoria, but who had a diverting brief fling with Catherine 'Skittles' Walters.

Old William Gladstone was not in sympathy with the wild life of the Prince of Wales, but understood how it stemmed from the idleness imposed by Victoria.

122

took her to Packington Hall, the Warwickshire seat of 'Sporting Joe' Aylesford, and his wife Edith, with whom Edward also had an understanding. After a few days they made an official visit to Coventry, with the Marquess of Hartington. Although it was a civic affair, the Duchess of Manchester was included in the party. Her liaison with Hartington was not, of course, common knowledge to the burgesses. Nor did they know, as the Prince did, of Hartington's previous involvement with Catherine Walters, a low-born but high-class courtesan from Liverpool universally known as 'Skittles', whom Hartington had set up in Mayfair with a superb establishment and a life pension of £2000 a year. Skittles, whose glamour was apparently enhanced by the occasional Scouse swear-words and obscenities she casually uttered, was a magnificent horsewoman and was accepted, to the great annoyance of the Duchess of Manchester, in the aristocratic hunts of Leicestershire and the West Midlands where Hartington also rode. Before his civic visit the Prince of Wales asked his equerry to make sure that the Mayor of Coventry conducted Hartington round a bowling alley in the town. Hartington, who displayed a perpetual air of sleepy boredom, indolently protested, but the Mayor insisted. 'Why?' asked Hartington. The Mayor, in all innocence, spoke according to his brief: 'His Royal Highness asked especially for its inclusion,' he explained, 'in tribute to your Lordship's love of skittles.' A bowling alley, incidentally, was not then solely a plebeian amusement. Edward had one at Sandringham, loved a game before he went to bed, and snared his guests into the bowling alley every Sunday night when the stroke of midnight ended the Sabbath.

During his premiership of 1870-1874, Gladstone tried hard to persuade the Queen to give the Prince of Wales more public responsibility in order to compensate for her own dangerous isolation from the nation. For a long time he worked on a proposal that the Prince should act as Viceroy of Ireland during the winter months, and live during the summer in Buckingham Palace, where he and Alexandra could carry out by proxy the social and formal activities desired of the Queen. When, after a succession of long memoranda, Victoria decisively vetoed this suggestion, it was proposed that the Prince should specialize in foreign affairs. But the Queen replied that her son was too indiscreet to be given access to ministerial secrets. Edward then conceived the idea of a State visit to India. The idea appealed to Disraeli, who had succeeded Gladstone as Prime Minister, and was nurturing a plan to consolidate imperialism by having Queen Victoria declared Empress of India. Disraeli therefore skilfully wheedled some quarter of a million pounds from the British and Indian Governments to finance the trip. Edward considered this a very mean subsidy, since he wished to make extravagant gifts of parallel prestige to the massive presentations of gold and jewels which the Indian Maharajahs were certain to make to him. But he took his chance and went.

Alexandra keenly wanted to make this journey with her husband, and if she had gone, the climax of the imminent scandal would not have been approached. But Edward was determined that she should not go, and, amid her tears—Disraeli said Alexandra behaved as if she were about to commit suttee—he finally left for Brindisi (via Paris) in October 1875. At Brindisi he boarded HMS *Serapis*, which was escorted by two frigates and the royal yacht *Osborne*.

The Prince of Wales took among his suite of eighteen Francis Knollys as private secretary and, as aides de camp, Prince Louis of Battenberg, father of the present Earl Mountbatten, and Lord Charles Beresford, a stormy sailor with a reputation for impetuous fearlessness in the hunting field and the boudoir. One of his equerries was his friend Lieutenant-Colonel Owen Williams, then commanding the Blues. He included, formally as the Queen's representative, 'cheery old Alfred'—Lord Alfred Paget, known as 'the best polo player in the kingdom'. The Queen approved this selection, possibly because he was a Paget, but more probably because, at the age of twenty-one, he had been the 'handsome young Calmuk-looking [slim] fellow' that she had once thought of

In this group of Edward's suite for his voyage to India, the Earl of Aylesford, the cuckolded 'Sporting Joe', is fourth from the left in the back row, wearing aide-de-camp's aiguilettes. Lord Carrington, who took over Nellie Clifden and other mistresses of the Prince including Hortense Schneider, is waiting for largesse seated at Edward's feet on the left, with Lord Charles Beresford right.

124

marrying before she fell for Albert—this despite a later characterization of old Alfred as 'a burly figure whom you were never astonished to encounter in localities and under circumstances which might have repelled a less inveterate Bohemian.'

But the Queen uttered violent objections to the three men in the suite listed merely as Edward's 'personal friends'. There would have been four, but 'Duppy' Dupplin had had to cry off. The three were Charles, Lord Carrington, Edward's legatee in love, George, the gambling, engine-driving Duke of Sutherland, and—most explosive of all, as the event proved—Sporting Joe Aylesford, of whom a contemporary thumb-nail portrait declared, 'Heneage Finch, Earl of Aylesford, a patron of the turf and of seven livings; orders his champagne from Charley Paris; considers himself absolved from his responsible duties in the House of Peers by the fact that his father-in-law dozed for eight-and-forty years on the benches of the House of Commons.' The reference half-concealed the most ominous fact in Aylesford's biography. His father-in-law was the father of Colonel Owen Williams. Aylesford's wife was Edith, née Williams, sister of the officer commanding the Blues.

The Duke of Sutherland took his piper. Alister had to compete with the Royal Marines band which, every evening aboard HMS *Serapis*, played 'The Roast Beef of Old England' to announce dinner and 'God Save The Queen' as the Prince of Wales entered the dining-cabin. This was separate from the wardroom, but three

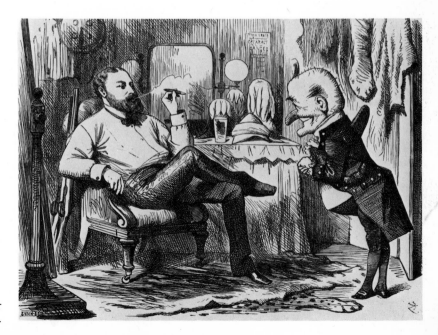

Praise from *Punch* for Edward's Indian tour.

125

naval officers were invited in rotation every night. All officers and civilians wore Duppy Dupplin's invention, the dinner-jacket, then a dark blue jacket with silk facings and Royal Household buttons, worn with black trousers and a black bow tie. The other invention of the voyage was deck tennis, adapted from lawn tennis and then played with normal balls (penalty for hitting a ball overboard: one sovereign).

The Indian tour was a triumphant political success, and was used, as Disraeli had planned, as the cue to proclaim Queen Victoria as Empress of India.[1] But the personal consequences for the Wales's, particularly for Princess Alexandra, were disastrous. Edward had left his 'wicked boys', Oliver Montagu and the Marquess of Blandford, behind. Montagu attended to the Princess of Wales. Blandford rashly paid over-passionate attentions to the Countess of Aylesford. Blandford was a sensitive, intelligent, but wild aristocrat of thirty-one who had married a daughter of the Duke of Abercorn and had three daughters. He had drawn into the 'fast' set centring on the Prince of Wales and the violent (and, candidly, disreputable) Earl of Aylesford, his younger brother, Lord Randolph Churchill. Randolph had been married for only eighteen months to Jennie Jerome, and their son Winston was then eleven months old. The passions—amorous, warlike, and in Randolph's case excessively blood-loyal—of these young men were to fire a sordid drama. Their youth was a factor: Aylesford and Randolph were only twenty-six and the Prince of Wales, the eldest of the set, was reaching thirty-four.

Edward had taken a fancy to pretty Lady Aylesford, and had written her some indiscreet letters.[2] Blandford, however, had fallen much more seriously in love with her, and she preferred him to the Prince. (Sporting Joe had a coarser taste, for the women he could pick up at the Cremorne Gardens.) With what was later considered some cynicism, Edward played Pandarus to the Blandford-Edith Aylesford infatuation by taking off the husband among his Indian suite. As soon as the royal party had sailed, Blandford moved his hunters and servants to a hunting-box conveniently near Lady Aylesford's home at Packington Hall, ostensibly for the start of the fox-hunting season. Lady Aylesford gave him a key to a private entrance to her home. The furtive visits began, and soon became open enough for the servants to complain. The lovers revolted

---

1 She immediately began signing letters V. R. & I.— Victoria Regina et Imperatrix— which considerably annoyed royal recipients within Europe, who considered the style appropriate only for 'communications east of Suez'.
2 It is always said, in extenuation, that these letters had been written 'many years before'. But Lady Aylesford had been married only four years. She had two children.

against the imposed stealth. In the consummation of their passion, Blandford resolved to abandon his wife and children permanently and Lady Aylesford wrote to her husband that she intended to elope with Blandford. She offered to delay the action until his return from India but vowed she would never again live with him as his wife. Blandford, at the same time, wrote to Edith's brother, Colonel Williams, who was with the Prince's party in India, saying that he was ready to meet Aylesford in a duel. Meanwhile another brother of Edith and Colonel Williams was seeking to fight a duel with Blandford, or, if he declined, to shoot him down like a dog in the street.

An unrehearsed incident on the Indian tour. Edward, utterly surprised by the tiger's spring, killed it with one shot.

This packet of letters reached the royal party in the middle of a forest in Nepal where a thousand elephants had been assembled for a lavishly organized tiger-shoot in honour of the Prince of Wales. The Prince called his former 'wicked boy' Blandford 'the greatest blackguard alive', climbed into his elephant-howdah and shot six tigers. Colonel Williams left the party on a doubly tragic errand: not only had he to try to stave off the imminent social disgrace, but his wife had also become seriously ill. Aylesford began the return trip to England shortly afterwards.

Blandford had been swiftly transformed, in the estimation of the Prince of Wales, into 'the greatest blackguard alive' not because he was an adulterer but because he was doing the one thing that Society would not tolerate. He was not covering up. In the reckless sincerity of his feelings he was provoking a public divorce action which would expose the activities of the Prince's set. Aylesford, in the Prince's eyes, became just as guilty. He stormed into London repeating the Prince's denunciation of Blandford, and swearing that he would divorce his wife and cite Blandford. Not only was a Divorce Court case the last thing that the Prince, as arbiter of elegant Society, wished, but this case in particular could result in the Prince himself being cited as a co-respondent, as was now being threatened, and at the least produce another cross-examination in court.

London Society itself knew every detail, but nothing official or specific had appeared in the newspapers. The most dangerous element in the imbroglio was the fiery attitude of Lord Randolph Churchill. Young Randolph had been an intimately affectionate friend of the Prince and for the moment still considered himself so. It had been Edward, in fact, who had brought off Randolph's marriage to Jennie Jerome, by persuading the Duke and Duchess of Marlborough to relax their opposition to the union of their son with an unknown American. (Years later, as King Edward the Seventh, he remarked that if it had not been for him, Winston Churchill would never have been born.) But Randolph's attitude was changing. It has been suggested that he was already jealous of a relationship between his wife and the Prince of Wales. This is unproven, and there is no evidence that the Prince and Lady Randolph were lovers before Winston's father had died. But, while Society hummed with the gossip, being even aware that detectives had been set to watch Blandford in case he should be shot down by Edith's brother, Lord Hartington on behalf of the Prince of Wales, and Prime Minister Disraeli on behalf of the Queen, were working with all devious power to keep the matter quiet.

French Society ladies *right,* found the corpulen Edward 'plus bath' (more attractive) than the dandies of the Garde

Right, overleaf, Tissot' *The Ball on Shipboard* exhibited in 1874 almost certainl represents Edward' famous party in honour o the Czarewitch of Russia given at Cowes aboard HMS *Ariadne* on 1 August 1873, when Lord Randolph Churchill me Jennie Jerome. [All th film and television presentations of this even make it a matter o feverish groping in th dark. The invitation card read, in fact: '3.30 to 7.3 P.M. DANCING.'] Th two girls i black-and-white ar wearing identical creation by Worth of Paris, th Jerome couturier, an Clara Jerome recorded how Princess Alexandr commented on the fac that Clara and Jenni Jerome used to wea identical dresses. Afte this 'ball' Edward and Alexandra alon encouraged the romanc between Randolph an Jennie. When Winsto Churchill was one o King Edward's Minister the King once said: 'If i had not been for me, tha young man would no have been in existence The Duke and Duches [of Marlborough] bot objected to Randolph' marriage. It was entirely owing to us that the gave way.

TU PARLES QU'IL EST
PLUS BATH
QU'ÉDOUARD!!!

There were thus three factions in London urgently concerned that there should be no divorce, and aware that the first step to block a divorce was to stop an elopement between Edith Aylesford and Blandford. First there was Blandford's family, its defence conducted by the distraught Duke and Duchess of Marlborough, who were close personal friends of the Queen, but vulnerable to the consequences of the independent sallies of the passionate Lord Randolph Churchill. There was Edith Aylesford's family, of whom Colonel Owen Williams was the most judicious, but always impeded by her ferociously talkative sisters and bloodthirsty brothers. And there was the Court, with the Queen knowing all but showing remarkable loyalty to her son.

Randolph had begged his brother not to elope. He failed to move him, but pressure on Lady Aylesford from her family convinced her of the bitter persecution she would endure if Society's code was transgressed. She faltered in her decision. The next step had been to stop Aylesford from initiating divorce proceedings. While Sporting Joe was still in India, Lord Randolph Churchill had telegraphed to the Prince of Wales, as his friend, asking him to use all possible influence on Aylesford. This plea was ignored, illogically and possibly mistakenly, by the Prince, who held at that early stage that he should not interfere in Aylesford's private decisions. Colonel Williams, in England, tried to persuade Aylesford that the matter could best be settled by Blandford's original suggestion: a duel between Aylesford and Blandford. This would be an illegal act which would have to take place abroad. But the actual power to stop a divorce lay with Lady Aylesford.

She gave to her lover Blandford the letters, with which she had previously teased him, written to her 'over-familiarly' by the Prince of Wales. Blandford gave the letters to Randolph. Randolph, all mature judgement blinded in his partisan campaign to stop the divorce, which was now refuelled by his repulsion from the Prince of Wales, saw the desperate light of political opportunity. 'I have the Crown of England in my pocket!' he said. He took the letters to Alexandra, Princess of Wales, who had tried so pathetically to be with her husband on this journey. He told her of the nature of the letters. He said—which was true—that the Solicitor-General, having read them, believed that their compromising character made it certain that, if a suit for divorce were proceeded with, the Prince would be called for cross-examination about their contents. He declared dramatically that their publication would provoke a reaction that would bar the Prince from succession to the throne. 'Publish these, and he will never sit upon the Throne of England!'

Theatre and music-hall were under Edward's keen patronage. He set up Lillie Langtry, left, on a stage career when he relinquished her as a mistress.

He wrote in the same strain to the Prince of Wales, no longer as a friend. Edward was then on the high seas returning from India, and the plainly threatening letter from Churchill was delivered to the unhappy Heir Apparent in Cairo. Edward did a brave thing. He ordered that copies of the letters should immediately be given to his mother the Queen and to his wife Alexandra, declaring that he had been indiscreet but guiltless. By doing so, he won his family to him. Queen Victoria even observed with a smile that letters were a family failing.

Now the Prince's mood changed from irritated uneasiness to blazing autocratic anger, and he turned like a tiger on Randolph Churchill. Accustomed to sycophancy, he had never been so bluntly and menacingly addressed in his life. Such words from Churchill tore an open wound in his self-esteem. With a lack of control equal to Randolph's, he sent Lord Charles Beresford speeding in the Royal yacht *Osborne* from Alexandria to Brindisi, thence overland to Calais and on to London. Beresford personally delivered to Churchill a summons from the Prince of Wales to come out and fight. It was a challenge to a duel with pistols. Beresford and Francis Knollys would support the Prince. Churchill was requested to name his seconds. The place suggested for the duel was on the north coast of France or Belgium, in the sand-dunes behind the Dunkirk-Ostend stretch.

Randolph replied in a letter which Beresford delivered to the Prince at Malta. Randolph's family believed then, and hold the tradition today, that he intended to fight a duel—he wanted Lord Falmouth as his second—but he could not lift his hand against a Prince of the Blood and wanted a deputy to be named by Edward. Those extracts of the letter which have been released only show that he declared the idea of a duel between a subject and the Sovereign's son to be unthinkable, and that no one was more clearly aware of that than the Prince of Wales.

George Spencer-Churchill, afterwards 8th Duke of Marlborough but always known as Blandford after his courtesy marquisate, eloped with Lady Aylesford while her husband 'Sporting Joe' was in India with Edward, who himself had dallied with Edith Aylesford in his time. The scandal cooked up from these ingredients was overpowering.

Aware that there would be no duel, the Prince of Wales prolonged his absence, dallying in Madrid and Lisbon. The machinery of Court pressure was exercised against Sporting Joe Aylesford. As the Prince sailed into the English Channel, London Society heard with the most profound relief that there would be no public scandal. Edward had asked that his wife Alexandra would sail out alone by yacht to board HMS *Serapis* off the Needles. After a private reunion they landed at Portsmouth to be greeted by their children and a welcoming party of Royals. They rode to the capital by train, made a carriage cavalcade through the streets of London, and, back at Marlborough House, went immediately to change into their most resplendent attire for an official appearance at Covent Garden Opera.

The opera was Verdi's *Un Ballo in Maschera,* the first performance of which had been witnessed by Edward in Rome. The gallery was full, but London Society knew that the Prince and Princess would be late, and did not bother to arrive until the middle of the second act. When they did deign to come, the men wore full decorations and, on the women, 'a more profuse display of diamonds has rarely been witnessed,' reported *The Times.* The party of the Prince and Princess of Wales entered the royal box. The whole assembly rose. There was an incredible ovation. Mademoiselle Albani, with full opera chorus, sang 'God Bless The Princes of Wales', and followed it with the National Anthem, in solo and chorus. Nobody thought of Verdi gnashing his teeth in Milan. Society was ecstatically aware that it had scraped through its worst crisis by the skin of its teeth.

Next day the Earl of Aylesford signed documents abandoning any divorce action against his wife and arranging a private deed of separation. Blandford took Edith Aylesford off to Paris, where they lived as Mr and Mrs Spencer and she bore him a son. Aylesford later attempted a further suit for divorce on this evidence, citing Blandford, but the Queen's Proctor intervened, alleging collusion by the three parties named and multiple adultery by the Earl of Aylesford. The adulteries were proved, but the divorce refused. Aylesford retired and died on a ranch in Texas. Blandford was divorced by his own wife, but refused to marry Edith, declaring that she was a remarkable mistress but impossible as the future Duchess of Marlborough. When she died, only Edward sent a wreath for her coffin. Lord Randolph Churchill and his wife Jennie were ostracized for eight years by the Prince of Wales, who let it be known that he would cut any person or family who received them socially. The Queen intervened and commanded Churchill to a Palace levée where the Prince of Wales was to represent her. But when Lord Randolph's name was called, Edward turned his back on him in front of the whole Court.

Almost immediately, Randolph and Jennie went on a long tour of the United States, before retiring into years of virtual exile in Ireland. The wife of Colonel Owen Williams of the Blues, left behind like Alexandra, died. One divorce was registered. Duppy Dupplin, who had asked to be excused from making the Indian trip with the Prince of Wales, had two motives for the request: he had beggared himself through trying to keep pace with his patron, and he was trying to save his marriage. He failed on both counts. On

Well corseted for riding at Blenheim, Jennie — Lady Randolph Churchill — went into exile but eventually again became a good friend of the Prince of Wales.

Lord Randolph Churchill was dragged into the Aylesford scandal through family loyalty, but bullied the Royal Family with Churchillian excess.

the day that Aylesford yielded to the enormous Establishment pressure not to divorce his wife, Lady Dupplin left the marital home to live with Herbert Flower, one of three famous hard-riding sportsmen in the Melton Mowbray hunting circuit. On the day Lord Randolph Churchill was persuaded to sign a humiliating letter of apology to the Prince and Princess of Wales, Lord Dupplin secured a divorce against his wife. The case was heard in Edinburgh and received very little publicity. He was twenty-seven years old, and nine years later he was dead. The Prince of Wales sent a wreath.

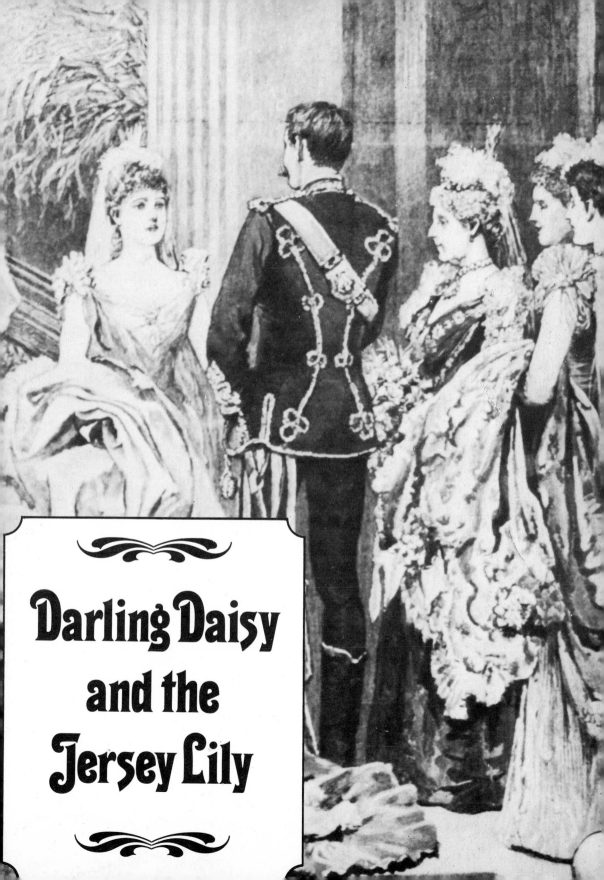

Darling Daisy
and the
Jersey Lily

M Y awful Dad'—'My darling Wife'. If Edward had found room, among the tremendous clutter of the ornaments at Sandringham, to hang a couple of poker-work mottoes over the billiard-room fireplace, they must have been these. *My Awful Dad* was his favourite farce and, certainly not without a twinge of delight at the implication of its title, he saw it whenever it was presented. It was the sort of piece that was performed by amateurs, and it was even put over by dashing young officers and colonels' ladies after a New Year's Day banquet he attended at Government House, Calcutta in 1876.

But it is all part of the filial game to slang one's father, and the second motto was more apt. The tribute to his wife, which he did not write but surely concurred with in all sincerity, was written

Victoria dressed her son in a multitude of uniforms, but never let him fight.

while he was on the Indian tour, in a bold skit published as a play called *Edward the Seventh*. The title itself showed no mean skill in prophecy. During the sixty years that he was Prince of Wales his mother officially referred to him as Albert Edward, and murmurously expected him to succeed to the throne as Albert Edward I. He kept the secret of his intention to take the Anglo-Saxon rather than the Coburg style until her death.

Edward the Seventh gives unexpected revelations of the rough attitude of literate public opinion to the unpopular Queen and her Germanic confidants, tilting especially at that time against her son, Prince Leopold, and her son-in-law, Prince Christian of Schleswig-Holstein, who had never fought even a skirmish but was promoted a British Major-General on the day he married Edward's younger sister Helena. The play, written in blank verse of varying quality, constantly refers to the Queen as a Guelph (the surname of the royal house of Hanover). When the Queen learns of a Press campaign for her abdication, she snorts:

> Bah! Am I not a Guelph? Did Guelph e'er yield
> To common sense or counsel? I'll reign on
> To spite them!

The Queen urgently pleads with her son 'Phleopold' to:

> Grow still liker that great one who's gone,
> More German, and more fond of German things. . . .
> See that the German influence grows apace.

And she mourns the antipathy to the German influence shown by the Heir Apparent:

> Alas, I would thy elder brother were
> As well-affected to that host as thou.
> He's kind and amiable to all but them,
> As though his blood were English every drop.

When the Prince of Wales, styled Prince Guelpho, enters, the Queen reproaches him for not spending enough time at his father's Mausoleum. The Prince replies, in a refreshingly contemporary catalogue of the royal chores:

> Who would then do the many acts of State
> I now perform? Who then would open parks,
> Lay corner-stones, hold levées, unveil statues.
> Preside at dinners, patronize the stage,
> Promote high art? . . .

And he follows this with the reference to his darling wife:

> For years, since, stretching your prerogative
> You have removed yourself from public life,
> Have I not in some measure ta'en your place,
> And, aided by my darling wife, the pet
> Of all the land, performed a regal part;
> Held drawing-rooms and levées, given balls,
> Gone here, there, everywhere throughout the shires,
> Promoting loyalty by gathering crowds,
> And giving them a show at which to gaze?
> And is it nought that in your noble name
> I've played the host to many Kingly guests?
> Been bored by ill-bred, savage visitors;
> Amused a Sultan, put up with a Shah,
> And entertained in turn a Royal tribe?
>
> Oh mother mine, 'tis no such easy task
> To play the host to order as I do,
> Whoe'er the guest, white, black, or good, or bad,
> Pleasant or otherwise, I've yet to wreathe
> The same bland smile about my lips; to press
> All hands the same; to embrace all cheeks the like;
> To vow how charmed I am; to laugh, to chat,
> To make them feel at home what time I wish
> That most of them were quite abroad; and then
> The programme of amusement; 'tis the same
> For all; its horrible monotony
> Has grown into a torture hard to bear;
>
> I know its every item. Item one—
> The visit to the Mansion House. Gross meats,
> Full-bodied wines, and fuller-bodied men;
> Excess exalted, ignorance enthroned,
> Cockney vulgarity apotheosized,
> And filthy Mammon made into a God;
> A Lord Mayor at your side for several hours,
> An Aldermanic vista 'fore your eyes,
> A plague of Common Councilmen around—
> Common's a word not nearly strong enough
> To qualify the fathers of the City—
> And then a floor knee-deep in mangled words,
> In wounded concords and in H's dropped. . . .

The play ends with the abdication of the Queen in favour of her son, who accepts the charge with much of the dutiful fervour of Henry V. And, as Prince Hal, he has already indulged his Falstaff. Indeed, burly Lord Alfred Paget, thinly disguised as 'Palstaff', sings an enlightening song about the reviving and rejuvenating influence of American ladies on English Society—the marriage of Jennie

Jerome to Lord Randolph Churchill had been the first of many fruitful unions of the old, inbred and possibly effete British aristocracy with the diamond-hard brilliance of American heiresses, and American debutantes haunted the Langham Hotel. The lyric has tricky rhymes, but its words are as pointed as Cole Porter's, and emphatic in their insistence that American girls are smarter and more enticing than their British cousins. The argument is well worth following:

L'Américaine

When you have suffered a season of parties,
    Waltzed with all Cockaigne's pale Gorgons and Graces,
Wondering where the confusion the heart is
    Under those breast-plates of muslins and laces,
Wondering whether the white shoulders you tickle,
    As your breath makes the loose ringlets gyrate,
Own aught but cold cream and powder as cuticle—
    Dine at the Langham at eight!

If we must all hang ourselves—try a new rope;
    Played out your Howards, de Veres, Montmorencies;
Gone to the wall old emasculate Europe,
    Worn out in sinews, in notions, and senses!
Where are your girls that can lure us and cozen—
    Be devilish, delicious, kind—cruel as fate—
Be women, in fact? If you'd flirt with a dozen—
    Dine at the Langham at eight!

L'Américaine! You may say that her manners
    Are free, that she brags, talks tall-ly and bounces,
Yet all the sweet scents of her own Savannahs
    Come out of her ringlets, her ribbons, and flounces.
Say that her nice nasal tone's an offence, or
    The way that she flirts is a tempting of fate;
Well, then, go and dine, immaculate censor—
    Dine at the Langham at eight!

There you will find them all, dear country cousins,
    Outshining native-bred spouses and sisters,
Flirting and eating and chatting by dozens,
    Their adjectives plain, their appetites—twisters,
Outré their dresses, outrageous, delightful,
    Making our women-folk wither with hate,
If you'd think all Bond Street dowdy and frightful—
    Dine at the Langham at eight!

The Prince of Wales, though he preferred his women safely married, did savour the 'devilish, delicious' lure of the *l'Américaine* when, as has been mentioned, he capitulated to the charms of Miss Chamberlayne, whom Alexandra unkindly called Chamberpots, possibly referring with only modified rapture to what was then the fashionable deep-bosomed figure. But this was the Princess's last open rebellion. From 1877, though she could still be secretly sore-wounded, she showed only the untarnished enamel of a consistent public role, that of the unconcerned *grande dame*, tolerant of her husband's voracious sexual appetite, openly accepting and receiving at least a proportion of his mistresses. She had five growing children. She was greatly involved in their domesticity and loved the family involvement; she was unaffectedly called by her children—and signed herself—'Motherdear' for all her long life. At the same time she relished her unchallenged position, *sans peur et sans reproche*, as the unblemished leader of a brilliant and 'correct' (if subcutaneously corrupt) Society. She was not intelligent, and her strong, simply-held religion was not evangelistic or condemnatory towards any writhing sinners around her. She had Oliver Montagu to proffer her pure courtly love. She was, as 'Prince Guelpho' had claimed, 'the pet of all the land.' She decided to present a personal, positive, sophisticated profile.

Alexandra first made this change of attitude evident when she received Lillie Langtry, Edward's first officially recognized mistress. Emilie Le Breton, daughter of the Dean of Jersey, wife of the prudently complaisant Edward Langtry, burst on to the London scene at the age of twenty-five in May 1877, when Alexandra was on a foreign visit, to her brother, the King of Greece. Slightly late, for other opportunists had succeeded before her—there was a remarkably communistic lack of exclusiveness about nineteenth-century amours—Edward grabbed her. And Alexandra entertained her with courtesy at Marlborough House.

It was an intense, but not particularly lasting, affair. Even while it flourished there were pauses for the enjoyment of others, like Patsy Cornwallis-West, the randy Irishwoman whose son became the second husband of Lady Randolph Churchill, who already had been more than friendly with the Prince of Wales; such was the convoluted character of the relationships of the time. And soon Edward was spending many weeks in France, where he conceived the political *entente cordiale* twenty-five years before he officially established it as king, and where he also became infatuated with the actress Sarah Bernhardt.

Sarah Bernhardt said, late in her life, 'I have been one of the great lovers of my century,' Edward, with a superior track-record, never bothered to register such a claim, having no theatrical con-

Alexandra 'showed the untarnished enamel of a consistent public rôle.'

'Motherdear' with the five children she bore Edward: Eddy, George, Louise, Victoria, Maud.

ception of the high romance of love. He was a compulsive social man, and for him social intercourse with women included sexual intercourse where possible. When Bernhardt came to London—her photographs at that time show a remarkable likeness to Greta Garbo—Edward cheerfully threw in all his harem to ensure the success of her gala French Fête at the Albert Hall. It was a kind of charity bazaar. The Prince bought a box of bonbons from Lillie Langtry. Alexandra bought two blue-eyed white kittens from Sarah Bernhardt. The Prince bought a self-portrait in oils of Sarah Bernhardt—she was a not inconsiderable artist—and dallied at her stall until she had taken £256. She did not perform in the theatre that night. Already she was recklessly under-rehearsing. She had written to her manager, crying off a *répétition*, 'I'm just back from the Prince of Wales at twenty past one and can't rehearse now. He has kept me since eleven'—interesting evidence of Edward's time-schedules.

The Prince had a deep practical interest in the stage. In Paris he was reputed to know the daily box-office takings of the most important theatres. In London he used his influence to launch Lillie Langtry, when they had become just good friends and only nostalgic lovers, on a stage career which brought her a fortune from

'I have been one of the greatest lovers of my century,' said the actress Sarah Bernhardt — and she tucked up Edward in bed on the stage in Paris before demonstrating her impact.

appearances in England and America. He went three times to her first play, and the world followed. In gratitude for the tolerance of the theatrical profession in accepting the beautiful, but embarrassingly gauche, Lillie, he gave a famous dinner party, which at that time had the impact of an accolade for a mixed list of actors, including Squire Bancroft, George Grossmith, Henry Irving, and Charles Wyndham, and aristocracy, including Carrington and, with Edward's very characteristic generosity to a fallen man, Sporting Joe Aylesford, shortly before his death.

But the Prince of Wales cherished also a secret wish to have been a professional actor. When he confessed this in Sarah Bernhardt's dressing-room in Paris during an interval of the tragedy *Fédora*, the high-spirited Sarah called for a costume and planted the Prince of Wales in a bed on the stage, where he lay for much of the last act shamming dead until the great Sarah entered to discover the corpse of her lover Vladimir, and extended her excruciatingly emotional finale as she kissed and crooned over the face of the appreciative Prince.

Edward's greater ambition had been to have experience as a professional warrior. Through the early decision of his parents this had been denied him: he was given the uniforms of honorary rank but never the active command, whereas his brother Arthur, Duke of Connaught, earned his rank by active service at least to brigade command. Consequently the Prince of Wales was remarkably sensitive to the not uncommon gibe[1] that, in spite of his Field Marshal's uniform, he had never fought in anything more dangerous than the annual Battle of Flowers at Cannes each spring. The shame was not sufficient to dissuade him from actually attending this revel: Princesse Jeanne de Sagan was often awaiting him there.

But Edward determined that his sons should experience the normal physical rigours of routine service in the armed forces of the Crown, preferably after enduring the education offered in an English public school, from which ordeal Edward had also been shielded. However, the elder son, Prince Eddy, was so intellectually backward, if sexually advanced, that he could not reliably be sent to Wellington, the new middle-class public school of which the Prince of Wales had become a governor. The younger, Prince George, though shy, was doggedly assiduous and of acceptable ability. Edward and Alexandra therefore decided to keep the two brothers together, first as naval cadets in the training-ship *Britannia*

---

1 Petty Service jealousy was so effective that, when the Prince of Wales's horse won the Grand Military Cup at Sandown races, he was disqualified on an objection that the race was open only to officers who had experienced active service.

at Dartmouth, where it was hoped that Eddy's diminished talent would not be noticed. They were later sent on three world cruises aboard HMS *Bacchante,* starting as midshipmen and, because of their size, nicknamed Herring and Sprat.

The Prince's genuine compassion for the underdog—even when he had put in a boot on the way down, as in the case of Aylesford—was matched by a rough justice which could act either democratically or autocratically, as it fitted his prejudices. On the Indian tour he had protested officially to the Foreign Office about what would be now called the counter-productive effect of the British officer-class contemptuously writing-off all the local population as 'niggers': 'Because a man has a black face and a different religion from our own, there is no reason why he should be treated as a brute.' With a rather skilful twist of the same upper-class invective, Edward crushingly deflated the Crown Prince of Germany, who protested at a London reception that he had had to yield precedence to the visiting King Kalakaua of Hawaii. The Prince chopped down his brother-in-law (who spoke idiomatic Establishment English) with the gem of logic: 'Either the brute is a king, or he's a common or garden nigger; and, if the latter, what's he doing here?'

King Kalakaua of Hawaii (which the Prince of Wales called the Sandwich Isles) was given royal precedence by Edward when he made a state visit to London.

The Prince of Wales also conducted a long but losing fight in favour of Colonel Valentine Baker, who had commanded Edward's own regiment, the 10th Hussars. Baker had been accused of kissing a girl in a first-class railway carriage. The impulsive incident had ended in Buster Keaton fashion. There were no carriage-corridors in those days and the couple arrived at Waterloo with the girl hanging outside on one running-board and the Colonel hanging outside on the other, shouting through the empty carriage that she could come in now because the momentary temptation had passed. Baker had been sent to jail for a year and dismissed from the Army. Later, through Edward's influence, he became Baker Pasha, a high officer in Egypt serving the Sultan of Turkey. When the British conquered Egypt, Edward strove to get Baker appointed Commander-in-Chief of the standing army of occupation. Puritan political forces got the appointment cancelled.

The Prince also, after a very long estrangement, not only warmly befriended but resolutely championed that spiky political personality Lord Randolph Churchill, and not only because of an interest in his wife. Moreover, he never relaxed his personal recognition and attachment to Churchill's predecessor as Leader of the House of Commons, Sir Charles Dilke, who had been submerged by Court and Parliamentary reaction to yet another Society divorce scandal.

Sir Charles Dilke, the Leader of the House of Commons who had to resign after a contrived divorce conspiracy, was never ostracised by the Prince of Wales.

Dilke had, in 1871, been an avowed Republican. Victoria loathed him. The Prince of Wales learned to respect him and became his friend. In return, Dilke briefed him in foreign affairs and candidly, though discreetly, worked to get for him access to Foreign Office telegrams. In 1885 Dilke was felled by a divorce case which had remarkable similarities to the Mordaunt case fifteen years earlier.

Mrs Donald Crawford, the sister of Dilke's brother's widow, told her husband, a Liberal Member of Parliament, that Sir Charles Dilke had long been her lover. Crawford, who had been receiving mysterious anonymous letters concerning his wife's fidelity, had been balefully pursuing a certain Captain Forster as the guilty party, which he probably was. But one morning he received an anonymous letter which, borrowing from the most outrageous dialogue of current melodrama, announced: 'Fool, looking for the cuckoo when he has flown, having defiled your nest. You have been vilely deceived, but you dare not touch the real traitor.'

Crawford immediately went to his wife's bedroom where an even more contrived interchange took place.

Mrs Crawford asked, 'Have you received the letter? What are its contents?' Crawford told her, and asked, 'Virginia, is it true that you have defiled my bed? I have been a faithful husband to you.'

'Yes,' said Mrs Crawford, 'it is true. It is time that you should know the truth. You have always been on the wrong track, suspecting people who are innocent, and you have never suspected the person who is guilty.'

'I never suspected anyone except Captain Forster.'

'It was not Captain Forster. The man who ruined me was Charles Dilke.'

Mrs Crawford then confessed to adultery with Dilke over four years, starting on her honeymoon, when she was eighteen. She named dates and various addresses, ranging from a shady house in Warren Street, Tottenham Court Road, to Bailey's Hotel in Kensington, and Dilke's own house in Sloane Street, 'where he taught me every French vice', including a few which Mrs Crawford was to detail with some relish in court when Crawford sued her for divorce naming Sir Charles Dilke as co-respondent.

Dilke claimed from the beginning that the case was a conspiracy, and proved that the circumstantial evidence was unsupportable: on the day that he was supposed to have first seduced Mrs Crawford, his political diary showed Foreign Office meetings, appearance on the Front Bench to answer Parliamentary questions, and even an attendance at a Palace levée. Dilke was therefore dismissed from the case as co-respondent, yet Crawford won his divorce against his wife on the ground of adultery although she had named no other. The Queen's Proctor accordingly stepped in and brought a further action designed to show that, since no adultery had been proved, Crawford's divorce should be dismissed. But the Queen's Proctor was a feeble advocate. He lost his intervention. The implication therefore was that Dilke *had* defiled the Crawford bed. He was forced to resign his place in the Government and to retire into private life. Edward never abandoned him. Although Dilke did eventually come back into political activity, Queen Victoria never recognized him. Only when Edward came to the throne did he, with the greatest possible publicity, command him to a levée.

Meanwhile Edward played the Devil at Cannes, wearing a scarlet cloak and horns in the Battle of Flowers, and fell in love with 'Darling Daisy' Brooke. It was to be the longest, and apparently the most passionate, love affair of his life, lasting more than ten years. It was also the most unwise of his many liaisons. In the normal fashion of that time, fine women, even when they had proud standing and, if not integrity, at least strong minds of their own, seem to have been distributed among the fast set almost like a decanter of port being given its ritual circuit round a club dining-table. But occasionally there arose an obstinate case of romantic love, which must be equated with an assertion of property rights. Darling Daisy had been the property of 'Charlie B.', Lord Charles Beresford, then a captain in the Royal Navy. Charlie B.'s policy with poachers had always been shoot to kill. But if property, or conjugal, rights had been a valid issue, perhaps more deference would have been paid to the lady's husband.

Darling Daisy was Lady Brooke, later Countess of Warwick, the wife of 'Brookie', Frederick Greville, styled Lord Brooke as heir to the Earl of Warwick and Brooke, whom he later succeeded. Daisy had been born Frances Maynard, heiress to a noble grandfather whose title did not pass in the female line although his massive fortune did. She grew into an astonishingly beautiful girl, and Queen Victoria had been anxious to marry her to her haemophiliac son, Prince Leopold. Leopold dutifully proposed when she was eighteen, but Daisy rejected Leopold and accepted Brookie on the same day. The Queen did not take mortal offence, and later invited her and her husband to stay at Windsor with some regularity. Brookie could not always accept. He had his own masculine sporting and sexual circuit, was something of a loner and explorer, and in fact later pioneered with Moreton Frewen the opening-up of Kenya.

Lord Charles Beresford had got into many a scrape with and without the Prince of Wales; it was he who had carried Edward's challenge to Randolph Churchill at the height of the Blandford affair. By 1889 his reputation in London had become somewhat too scorching, and he took the advice of the Prince and others to leave the House of Parliament, and London Society, and resume his previously gallant and successful career in the Navy. In an intoxication of reform he crowned his conversion by becoming reconciled to his wife, who was considerably his senior, but he did not tell Darling Daisy. The first that Lady Brooke heard of the resumption of domestic bliss was the incredible news that Lady Charles Beresford was pregnant after lying ten years fallow. Appalled by Charlie's infidelity to *her*, Daisy wrote him an excoriating letter of reproach. The sailor was away at sea at the time, and Lady Charles opened it. Fearing that, if her husband did read it, he might be tempted back to Daisy, she told him nothing of it but entrusted it to the Society solicitor George Lewis, whose strongroom was crammed with the metal boxes enclosing the scandals of the aristocracy. Lady Charles requested Mr Lewis to convey to Lady

'Darling Daisy', Frances
Lady Brooke and
afterwards Countess of
Warwick, was the most
sensuous mistress of the
Prince of Wales.

Lady Charles Beresford
was understandably
annoyed when she opened
a letter from her
husband's mistress
reproaching him for his
infidelity in having
intercourse with his wife.

Fiery Lord Charles
Beresford came home
from sea and struck the
Prince of Wales as 'a
cowardly blackguard.'

Brooke that there was no immorality or even lack of taste involved in a man's impregnating his own wife, and it would be appreciated if Lady Brooke sent no more letters to Lord Charles Beresford.

Daisy now knew that her letter had miscarried and was in a lawyer's hands. She determined that she must get it back. She appealed to the Prince of Wales, on the basis of their friendship of rapidly increasing ardour and of his position as arbiter of Society. Edward went to Lewis who, with amazing indiscretion, let him read the letter but not destroy it. The Prince then called repeatedly on Lady Charles to ask for the letter to be returned to its sender. Lady Charles realized that the Prince and her hated rival Lady Brooke were now lovers, and declined to give up a weapon that might yet destroy Daisy for ever. The Prince of Wales cut Lady Charles and ordained that this ostracism should be observed by all his friends. Charlie B. came home from sea, aware at last that the embarrassing letter existed, but now far more consumed with a burning rage against the Prince of Wales for the social banishment of his wife, and a rending sexual jealousy against him for taking his place in the arms of Lady Brooke. In a violently angry interview at Marlborough House, Lord Charles not only raised his hand against his

former bosom friend and the heir to the throne, he brought it heavily down. He struck the Prince as he called him a cowardly blackguard, and went back to sea with his *lèse-majesté* completed. The Prince of Wales pronounced with even more emphasis the excommunication of Lord and Lady Charles Beresford.

There was a phrase of doom then current in upper-class conversation which has now lost its impact. The term was 'social death', and it meant almost literally what it said. By a curious coincidence the advance of social death now began to push forward on two fronts, both impelled by the Prince of Wales. For the Tranby Croft Baccarat Scandal was about to break.

This affair was far more of a sensation in 1891 than it could ever be now. During the Doncaster race meeting of the previous autumn the Prince had hoped to pass the week with Lady Brooke at the house of a mutual friend, from which he could drive by day to see the St Leger and the other races. By a succession of accidents this plan was not carried through, and a house-party was hurriedly made up at Tranby Croft, the Yorkshire home of a possibly *parvenu* ship-owner, Arthur Wilson.

On two successive nights when, according to the Prince's wish, the illegal card-game of baccarat was being played, the son of the house saw one of the principal guests cheating the banker, who was the Prince of Wales, of some £225 by fiddling his counters after the cards were dealt. The player involved was Sir William Gordon-Cumming, Baronet, Officer Commanding the Scots Guards, and long the Prince's friend. Altogether, five witnesses confirmed this, and they reported what they had seen to two older guests, Lord Coventry and General Owen Williams, the brother of Edith Aylesford.

These gentlemen thought they could keep the Prince of Wales out of any ensuing scandal by threatening to expose Gordon-Cumming immediately unless he signed what was virtually a confession of guilt and left the house at dawn. He concurred, after observing miserably that he would be exposed in any case if the Prince of Wales cut him at any future meeting. His instinct was correct, and in order to still mounting gossip Gordon-Cumming sought to clear his character by bringing an action for libel against the five young witnesses who had first reported alleged cheating to Coventry and Williams.

The Prince's agents went to extraordinarily devious and questionable lengths to try to prevent this case coming to court, since they rightly assumed that the real prisoner in the dock, in the view of the anti-royalist Press and the Nonconformist British conscience,

The Noncornformist
Conscience was appalled
by the Baccarat Scandal at
the house-party at Tranby
Croft, where Sir William
Gordon-Cumming is seen
next to the Prince of
Wales.

The Lord Chief Justice, Lord Coleridge, presiding over the Baccarat Trial.

would be the Prince of Wales, who nightly indulged in illegal gambling. These efforts failed, however, and the case came for trial from 1 to 9 June 1891. The case was tried by the Lord Chief Justice, Lord Coleridge, who jeopardized his reputation for impartiality by taking the Prince's son Eddy, by now created Duke of Clarence, to dinner on the first night of the trial. But Coleridge could not protect Edward from a vitriolic attack by Counsel for Cumming, who suggested that the Colonel had nobly sacrificed himself by signing a paper to save the Prince of Wales from public obloquy over his gambling propensities 'to save a tottering throne and prop a falling dynasty'.

When Colonel Gordon-Cumming gave evidence rebutting the allegation that he had cheated the Prince of Wales at cards, Edward, for many years his friend, gazed stonily ahead. Edward's evidence was: 'The charges seemed so unanimous that there was no other course open but to believe them.'

Dramatic though the words were, they represented the militant wing of public reaction to so-called 'revelations', feeble though they might be, which seriously put in question among the more hypocritical newspapers the suitability of allowing the Black Queen to be succeeded by a prince who played cards for money. Edward, with his normal courage, sat publicly in court throughout the trial when he could have been skulking at Chiswick, and publicly endured the most concentrated churchified opposition to him that had yet been launched. As for the case itself, the libel suit by Gordon-Cumming was lost after fifteen minutes' consideration by the jury.

The effect on Lieutenant-Colonel Gordon-Cumming was catastrophic. He was guilty, but in a moral sense the Prince of Wales was as guilty for gambling with men who could not afford to lose, and ruining them as he ruined, for other social reasons, Duppy Dupplin, Christopher Sykes, and even Daisy Brooke, who eventually could not stand the financial load of entertaining him. In one day Gordon-Cumming was dismissed from the Army, expelled from all his clubs, and exiled to his bare estate in Scotland; a fate which he only ameliorated by marrying, in the morning of that very day, a rich American lady.

Lieut.-Col. Sir William Gordon-Cumming, Bart., soldier and cardsharper. Many players cheated when faced with the high stakes imposed by the Prince of Wales.

But it was 'social death', as *The Times* primly reminded its readers, taking a back-hander at the unpopular Arthur Wilsons who had invited the party to Tranby Croft:

> When a man dies physically, those who have to do with him remain in retirement for a time. Those can hardly do less who are indirectly responsible for this far more tragic calamity, the ruin of a fine career. . . .
>
> [Gordon-Cumming] is, in fact, condemned by the verdict of the jury to social extinction; his brilliant record is wiped out; and he must, so to speak, begin life again. Such is the inexorable social rule. A man who defrauds the friends whom he meets at the card table has forfeited his honour. He has committed a *mortal offence;* society can know him no more.

This statement was valid for Lieutenant-Colonel Sir William Gordon-Cumming, and it was equally valid for Lord and Lady Charles Beresford. They had not even played baccarat, but they had offended the Prince of Wales. Lord Charles was comparatively immune in the Mediterranean. But social death' struck Lady Charles so hard, with the rigid ostracism she endured from anyone who expected a future favour from the Prince of Wales, that in the middle of the Tranby Croft case she put her London house up for sale and made preparations to live abroad to escape further humiliation.

Fighting Charlie B., mortified at the treatment being meted to his wife, stated publicly within Society, though not yet in print, that since it was now inadmissible to fight the Prince of Wales in a duel he would use the modern weapon, publicity. His wife, with the feminine ruthlessness that pays no respect to club conventions, told the Prince of Wales, through the Prime Minister, that publication of the present sexual scandal, following the sensation of the Tranby Croft case, would damage his reputation for ever. A sister of Lady Charles then prepared a printed version of the sexual life of Lady Brooke for publication under the title *Lady River,* and it began to be circulated. Lady Charles Beresford, by now an obsessive termagant with whom it was impossible to reason, threatened the Prime Minister with the blackmail of this publication and assured him dramatically, 'People are beginning to ask themselves how much more evil the Prince of Wales will work in an endeavour to deteriorate Society.'

The affair burned on for nine months more before acceptable assurances of polite regret were exchanged. By this time Gladstone was tottering into the premiership again, and brightly suggested that a solution of all the public-relations difficulties might be for the Queen to abdicate (twenty years after such a panacea had first been mooted). The Prince was passing fifty, and had not yet been given the opportunity to handle a key to the Foreign Office boxes. But Edward echoed his mother's laughter, and planned the tactics of his next sortie in the Battle of Flowers.

The Battle of Flowers at Cannes, constantly attended by the Prince of Wales, was his most dangerous active service.

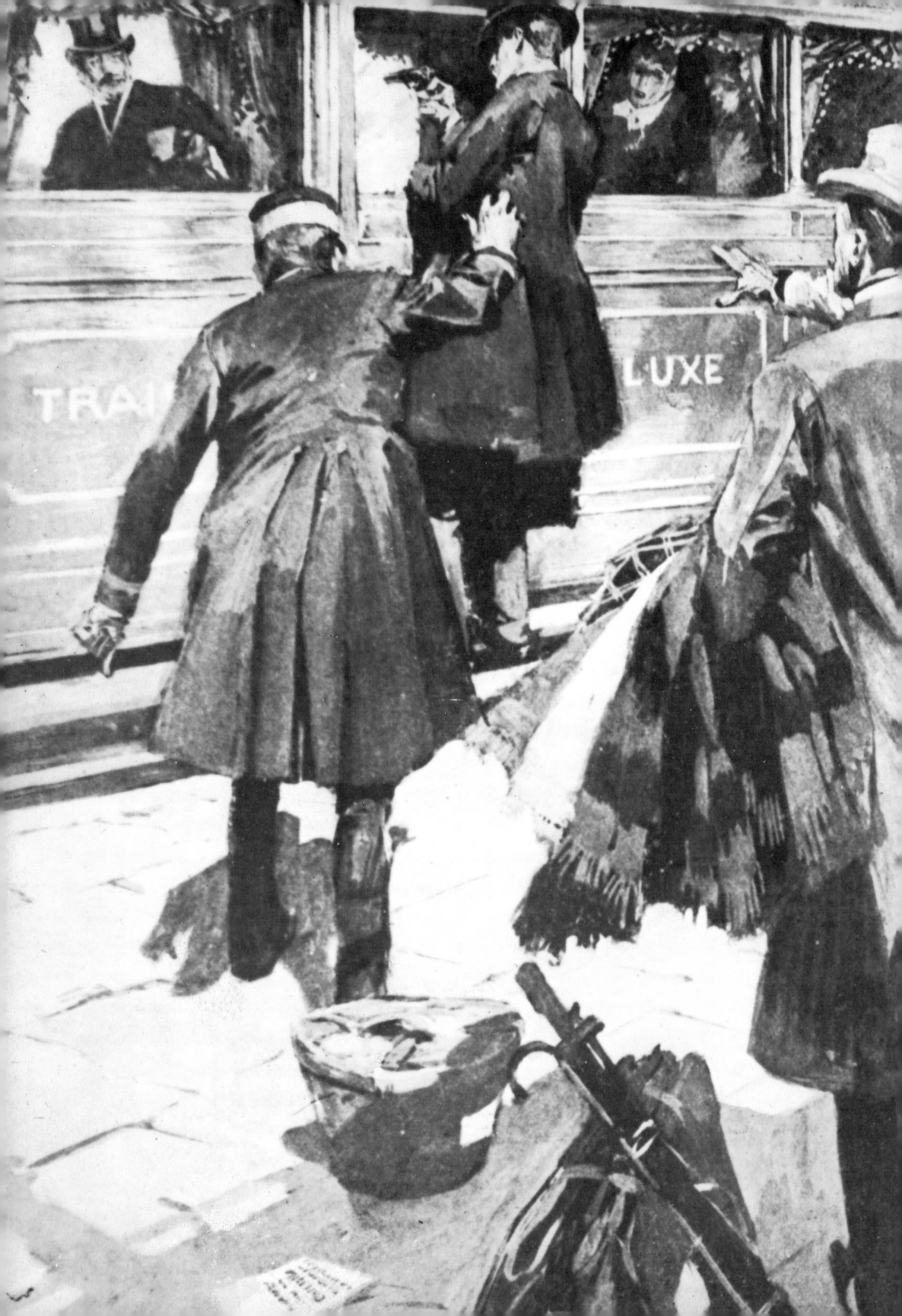
TRAI
LUXE

A Dangerous Profession

T the height of the long Beresford scandal, Edward slipped away to Paris for one of the diversions he found so necessary, and was chatting at ease in the green-room of the Comédie Française. The French actress Judic, not unaware of his vexations in London, suggested, 'You should settle in France, Sir. And it would make Royalty popular here.' Edward reflected for a moment on the executions, exiles, abdications, and dethronements, that France had awarded its despots in one century, and declined with twinkling eyes. 'Thank you—but you use up your Kings at too fast a rate in this country.' He was soon to know that heirs to the throne were also expendable.

In Paris he was inevitably the target of London newspaper gossip. If the Opposition Press could not, at any particular moment, sniff out anything against his morality, they could always exaggerate his debts. Ever since the nation had had continuously to bail out the Prince of Wales who became George IV, 'the debts of the Prince of Wales' had become a sort of myth in the public mind, which could always be raised by the gutter Press as a burning issue in slack times, like 'the Yellow Peril'. The truth was that Albert Edward, Prince of Wales, was occasionally financially embarrassed by his high rate of living, but also because of the extravagance of the State duties which the Queen expected him to perform without paying him a penny towards his outlay. But he jogged on without public scandal, and eventually had advisers who put him straight.

Gaslight, girls, and gaiety always round the corner: the lure of the boulevards of Paris, which Edward once described to Parisians as 'your beautiful city where I have always felt at home.'

Right, overleaf. Prince Albert Victor, Edward's son Eddy Duke of Clarence, a dissipated young man who died early and relieved Britain of a rotten future King, seen opposite his unconventional contemporary Marie Lloyd.

French Oyster

E. Thos

EDOUARD VII

EDOUARD VII

Long live our Sovereign,
England's King!
Shakespeare

EDWARD VII.
BORN 1841.
ASCENDED
THE THRONE
JAN. 22nd 1901.
CROWNED
JUNE 26.1902.

COIN OF THE REIGN
EDWARD VII.

GREAT
SEAL
EDWARD VII

RAPHAEL TUCK & SONS' "KINGS & QUEENS OF ENGLAND" SERIES 617
Designed in England Chromographed in Germany

Some of these were Jews, notably the Rothschilds, the Sassoons, and Baron Hirsch, and all were understandably rich; if they could not ensure that their own fortunes prospered, how could they order the affairs of the Prince? But it would be idle to assert that Edward chose his friends for their capital rather than their character. As Prince of Wales and king, he opened the windows of stuffy Society to the invigorating draught of fresh minds and fresh enthusiasm, often from ethnic groups which the old aristocracy despised. He was scorned for cultivating Americans as well as Jews, businessmen as well as tycoons of the turf.

In Paris, where he stayed as usual in his suite at the Hôtel Bristol, Edward was besieged by moneylenders' touts, who became such a nuisance that, after a complaint through the British Ambassador, the French police made a sweep and arrested most of them as vagrants. But the same situation would occur at Cannes or Homburg or Marienbad. Fuchs and Schwartz, the two great Viennese moneylenders, certainly pestered him at Homburg, and one of them had a German countess on his pay-roll whose duty it was from time to time to sound the Prince on his inclination to borrow.

Other ladies were more cordially generous, especially after his accession. At Marienbad a high-class whore announced that she had come post-haste from Vienna to be granted the opportunity of sleeping with the King. When his equerry said that this could not be arranged, she replied that, if it came to the worst, she would sleep with *him* rather than waste her fare.

Edward returned from the Continent to face the growing problem of his elder son. Prince Eddy had left the Navy, had been created Duke of Clarence and Avondale, was sent for a short spell to Cambridge, where, surely in derision, he was given the degree of Doctor of Law, and then joined the Army, which he disliked in spite of a promotion to Lieutenant-Colonel. His social behaviour was so dissipated, and his weakness for women so marked, that the Prince of Wales saw no alternative but to exile him to the Colonies as a sort of short-term remittance-man. Princess Alexandra and Queen Victoria, however, preferred the old remedy of an early marriage. Prince Eddy had already proposed to Princesse Hélène d'Orléans, daughter of the Pretender to the French throne. But the Pope refused to allow her to abandon Roman Catholicism, and the matter was speedily hushed up before the dour and bigoted British public caught a hint that the heir to the Heir Apparent was contemplating a Catholic wife.

Queen Victoria then put forward the name of Princess May of Teck. She was the daughter of the Lady Mary Cambridge about

Left, overleaf. 'Put me among the girls' was Edward's song, whether at the Bal Tabarin in Paris, the Palace Theatre in London, (chorus-line on review), or as King of Clubs on the look-out for a Queen of Hearts.

Left. Millions of Coronation Mugs carried, like the postcard here, the wrong date for Edward's Coronation. Intended for 26 June 1902, the ceremony had to be cancelled when he underwent an emergency operation for peritonitis on 24 June.

whom the Queen (and, at least in lip-service, Alexandra) had earlier been so scathing for her flirtatious and tomboyish behaviour. Lady Mary had finally been married off to Prince Francis of Teck, anglicized as the Duke of Teck, and popularized as 'Bif-Teck'. Their daughter May accordingly became engaged to the Duke of Clarence, with no great willingness on either side. Within six weeks, however, Eddy died suddenly of pneumonia. His brother, Prince George, rose immediately into the direct line of succession to the throne as Duke of York, and it was decided that Princess May should become his wife. This marriage duly took place in the

Princess May of Teck, daughter of Victoria's tom-boy cousin Lady Mary Cambridge, was compulsorily engaged to marry Edward's eldest son and reform him. The prospective bridegroom died, and she was accordingly married to Edward's second son, Prince George.

teeth of a virulent attack on Princess May from, of all quarters, a Radical newspaper, on account of a supposed morganatic taint in the ancestry of her father: 'If Teck went to visit the most insignificant princeling of pure blood, he would not be asked to sit down.' A year after the marriage, in June 1894, their eldest son David was born, who later became King Edward VIII. Their second son Albert was born eighteen months later. Thus the unforeseen events of four years in the 1890s put together on to the British stage five generations of Sovereign Emperors: Victoria, Edward VII, George V, Edward VIII and George VI.

Four generations of British Sovereigns. The future Edward VIII in the arms of his great-grandmother Queen Victoria, flanked by the future Edward VII and George V. The picture was taken in 1894 when the subjects were aged respectively two months, 75, 52 and 29 years.

Edward's surviving son was of a very different character from
himself. The future King George V was retiring and diffident,
though with a strong sense of duty. With admirable understanding,
Edward was never over-bearing; he always said that the relationship
was that of brothers rather than father and son, and George wrote
in his diary on his father's death that they had never had a cross
word. Edward wrote to the Duke of York frequently and openly
during their absences, never masking the identity of his lady
companions even if he was discreet about their activities.

Having secured the succession, Albert Edward Guelph had little
to do until his own accession except to follow the social tram-tracks
on which he had been placed for so long, while exercising the
individuality of his temperament when he could. He diligently
supported the theatre, and did not shrink from favouring the comics
of the music-halls, though in later years preferably in Paris rather
than London. He patronized Society bazaars, yet checked the
rapaciousness of some of the débutantes and actresses who twisted
too hard in their extortion. At a Fancy Fair at the Albert Hall he
patiently asked at a refreshment stall for a cup of tea, which was
offered at an artificially high price. The young flirt who served him
skittishly took a sip from the cup, and said, 'Now the cup of tea is
five guineas.' He quietly passed five guineas over, then handed back
the tea and asked, 'Will you give me a clean cup?'

At Homburg, where he took an annual dieting cure, he broke his
fast more often than not by darting off to intimate dinners at
Frankfurt followed by a visit to the Opera House. He delighted in

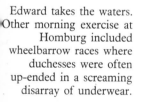

Edward takes the waters.
Other morning exercise at
Homburg included
wheelbarrow races where
duchesses were often
up-ended in a screaming
disarray of underwear.

The

La Goulue, the uninhibited dancer at the Moulin Rouge in Paris. When Edward came into the music hall she shouted from the stage 'Ullo, Wales! Are you going to pay for my champagne?' Edward chuckled and ordered champagne for all the dancers and the band.

the galaxy of English and American young beauties who congregated there, with no real need for slimming at all, but he appreciated most the wheelbarrow races where duchesses were often up-ended in a screaming disarray of underwear. He was always a man for a romp: at Sandringham he even proved handy with a fire-hose played on surprised and grimly-cackling guests. In the Paris theatres the reserved double-box was always furnished with special armchairs sent down from the Hôtel Bristol to receive the ample backside of their favourite patron. La Goulue, the *femme fatale* of Toulouse-Lautrec, interrupted a show at the Moulin Rouge to shout when Edward came in: 'Ullo Wales!' *Est-ce que tu vas payer mon champagne?*' And Wales cheerfully settled the bill for the dancer. At the age of fifty he decided that he was too fat to waltz, and promptly gave up dancing altogether, except for quadrilles on State occasions, and at the magnificent Fancy Dress Ball given by Louisa, now triumphantly Duchess of Devonshire, in the year of the Queen's Diamond Jubilee.

Attractive women were sent to the spas by Viennese moneylenders to offer loans to needy nobility and royalty.

As a dealer not only in social death but in social niceties, Edward sobered up High Society by discouraging after-dinner drinking. By his example he was probably the best propagandist for cigarette-smoking. His brands were Royal Derbies, Laurens, and Dembergi's Egyptian. His cigars, smoked by the dozen a day, were Henry Clay Tsars and Corona y Coronas. He virtually invented a cocktail, which he called his 'short drink'. Its recipe was as well known as the Lord's Prayer to the barmen of every club he frequented. The ingredients were rye whisky, crushed ice, a small square of pineapple, Angostura bitters, lemon peel, maraschino, champagne and powdered sugar; it would be worth a king's ransom to surrender the secret of the actual proportions.

This active prince, in a single year, spent two days a week on State functions, sailed his huge racing cutter, raised money for hospitals which were then all voluntarily supported, went to the theatre or opera twice a week, entertained a hundred foreign and colonial princes, shot on forty-three days of the year and went racing on another fifty-three, won the Derby, gave his annual dinner to the Jockey Club that night in celebration, and took the Countess of Dudley to bed to prolong the festivity until dawn. He was fifty-three. She, by a further strange convolution of relationships, was Georgiana, born Moncrieffe of that Ilk, the sister of

Georgiana Countess of Dudley, whom Edward took to bed after the Jockey Club celebration of his first Derby win in 1896. She was the sister of Harriett Mordaunt.

Edward made Derby Day a royal occasion, and won the race twice.

176

Harriett Mordaunt, and the second wife (though thirty years younger) of that William, Lord Ward, later advanced to Earl of Dudley, who had thrown out on the street his pregnant wife Constance, whom young Lord Dupplin had loved.

The Prince of Wales was also shot at by an assassin, who missed, but was captured by the police at Brussels railway station, where the attempt occurred on 14 April 1900. Echoing the famous exhortation of the French Empress Eugénie when Orsini threw a bomb and hit the wrong carriage—'Don't bother about us. Such things are our profession. Look after the wounded'—Edward made light of the experience until he discovered in great wrath that the British Parliament had no intention of sending him a message congratulating him on his escape. It was all great training for the kingship he was to assume within a few months.

In his sixtieth year his hour had come. He threw back the

King Edward precedes
the German Kaiser as
they follow his mother's
coffin into Paddington
Station before the burial
at Windsor.

shutters to flush out the gloom from a thousand rooms in Windsor Castle and Balmoral. He tipped out his mother's cobwebbed souvenirs and methodically smashed to pieces her statues of John Brown. And, as he examined the exhilarating private fortune which her frugal spending had accumulated, and added the gems in her personal gift to the hereditary Crown Jewels being re-set for the coronation, he prepared, with the mood of the nation behind him, to begin a reign of splendour. As his cousin Alfonso of Spain declared, 'Being a king is a dangerous profession. But it is devilish well paid.'

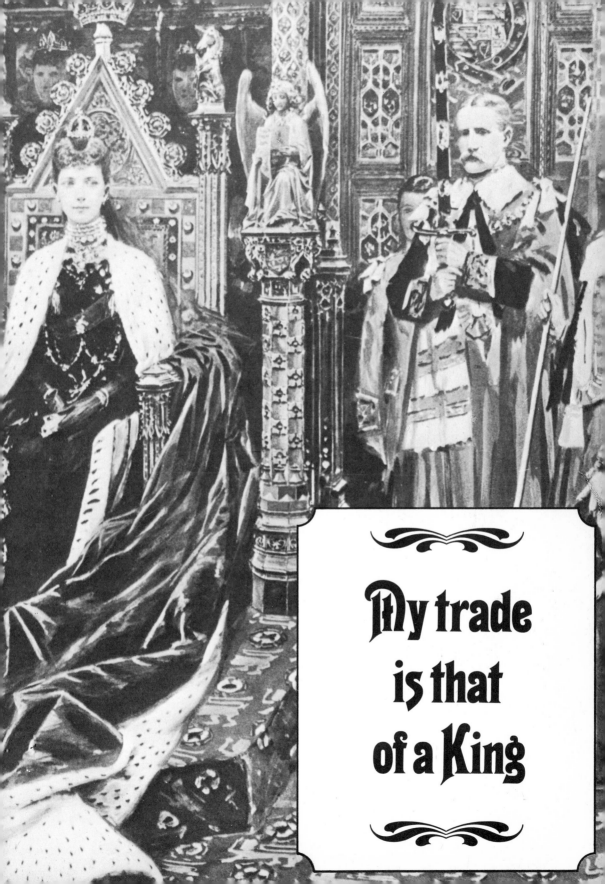

My trade
is that
of a King

O N 21 January 1901 all that the nation owed the Prince of Wales was accommodation in four rooms in Windsor Castle—Rooms 238, 239, 240 and 241— which his mother graciously allowed him. On 22 January, when Queen Victoria died and he became King Edward the Seventh,[1] he inherited the Sovereignty of Great Britain, Ireland, along with the Empire of India and the British Dominions beyond the Seas. The next man to fire a revolver at him would not be taken so lightly. As Edward explained to ministers who wished him to recognize the new Karageorgević regime in Serbia after the murder of King Alexander and the extermination of the Obrenović dynasty, 'Mon métier à moi est d'être Roi. My trade is that of King. King Alexander was also by his métier un Roi. As you see, we belonged to the same guild, like labourers or professional men. I cannot be indifferent to the assassination of a member of my profession, or, if you like, of my trade union. We should be obliged to shut up business if we, the Kings, were to consider the assassination of Kings as of no consequence at all. I regret, but you see that I cannot do what you wish me to do.'

Idylls of the King at Marienbad: pouter-bosoms and close-ranked detectives.

King Edward and Queen Alexandra open Parliament within a month of their accession.

The man's self-importance, which had never been slight, was growing. But his follies diminished, as could be expected in any man over sixty. He did not renounce mistresses, nor, if the informed opinion of the next generation is to be credited, did he lack virility. The daughter of his most wise, gentle and faithful friend, Alice Keppel, began her biography: 'Mamma used to tell me that she celebrated the Relief of Mafeking [18 May 1900] sitting astride a lion in Trafalgar Square. I was born a fortnight later.' And the author, Sonia Keppel, who had the best of advice, boldly entitled her life-story *Edwardian Daughter* (London, 1959).

Edward did not relinquish feminine entertainment, as Sophie Hall-Walker realized at Marienbad when the King requested that she should bring in for his after-dinner relaxation Maud Allan, a dancer who wore 'only two oyster shells and a five-franc piece'; nor did he renounce feminine comfort, which was all that the discreet Agnes Keyser, who founded King Edward's Hospital for Officers, ever admitted was given to the Patron who visited her so frequently. But he did grow in discretion. When he visited Copenhagen he sent an equerry to the reigning beauty explaining with the utmost tact that, following his strict protocol, he ought not to visit her since he would not have the reserves of time and energy to visit her recently-displaced rival.

---

1 He gracefully told the Accession Assembly of his Privy Council that he did not belittle the name of Albert, but the example of his father had convinced him that there could be only one Albert, and he would take the name of Edward in which he had six English predecessors.

Mrs Alice Keppel, most tactful and politically influential of all Edward's mistresses, was invited by Queen Alexandra to go to the bedside of the dying King.

In later years Edward did not often ride, in consideration of his weight and girth. But at Sandringham he occasionally crushed his favourite pony.

Kind Edward at Biarritz, where he enjoyed the privacy he was never granted in England to savour a quiet stroll by the sea.

And he grew in charity. He had always been beneficent, but now he took perhaps a more personal interest in the people who received his alms. He had become astonishingly fond of Biarritz as an invigorating retreat from the English winter. Every day, as he left his house there for a walk before lunch to the sea, two blind beggars stationed themselves at the gate, and held out their bowls as they heard the King's fox-terrier Caesar[1] barking. King Edward would drop his gifts into the bowls with the assurance, 'Until tomorrow.' One day he was disturbed to find that one of the beggars was missing. Next day the pair were reunited.

1 Caesar had the inscription on his collar: 'I am Caesar, the King's dog.' It was less haughty than Pope's famous crest for the collar of the spaniel he gave to Frederick, Prince of Wales, the son of King George II:

'I am His Highness' dog at Kew.
Pray tell me, Sir, whose dog are you?'

King Edward and his fox-terrier Caesar. At Edward's funeral Caesar, led by a Highland servant, followed the coffin on the gun-carriage in advance of the German Emperor.

Edward said to the absentee blind man of the previous day, 'Where were you yesterday?'

'I beg your pardon, Monsieur le Roi.'

'Were you ill?'

'No, Monsieur le Roi.'

'Then you were late.'

'No, Monsieur le Roi.'

'What, then?'

'Excuse me, Monsieur le Roi. I beg your pardon. You were early.'

'A thousand apologies!'

One final story on that note, and the King is dead. Mrs Leah Kersh, the mother of the late Gerald Kersh who died in New York, and of the young Cyril Kersh who is living in London, was wheeling a pram along the sea-front at Hove, the classier end of Brighton, when she was stopped by a solitary stout gentleman whom she recognized as the King.

'What a beautiful baby!' he said. 'May I look more closely?'

She drew back and he looked under the sunshade.

'You must be a very proud mother,' he said. 'Would you allow me to give you a portrait of *my* mother?' He felt in his pocket and gave her a golden sovereign, bearing the head of Queen Victoria.

On the afternoon of Friday, 6 May 1910, King Edward was dying in Buckingham Palace. Queen Alexandra sent for Alice Keppel, who came to the Palace and was taken into the King's bedroom to say good-bye to him. Before midnight he was dead. Nine kings headed 1200 distinguished mourners at his funeral. Queen Alexandra was magnificently calm and, in a transcendental manner, somehow happy. 'After all,' she said, 'he always loved me the best.'

Acknowledgements

The words of British Royalty, when written and registered, are reproduced by gracious permission of Her Majesty Queen Elizabeth II in:

Georgina Battiscombe, *Queen Alexandra*, London, 1959.
Roger Fulford, *Dearest Child*, London, 1964.
Roger Fulford, *Dearest Mama*, London, 1968.
Elizabeth Longford, *Victoria R.I.*, London, 1964.
Philip Magnus, *King Edward the Seventh*, London, 1964.
Cecil Woodham-Smith, *Queen Victoria 1819-1861*, London, 1972.

A short list of works which have thrown light on this period is:

Allen Andrews, *The Splendid Pauper*, London & New York, 1968.
Samuel Beeton, Aglen Dowty, S. R. Emerson, *The coming K___*, London, 1872.
Samuel Beeton, Aglen Dowty, Evelyn Jerrold, *Edward the Seventh*, London, 1876.
Denis A. Bingham, *Recollections of Paris*, London, 1896.
Charles Bradlaugh, *George Prince of Wales*, London, 1870.
Countess of Cardigan, *My Recollections*, London, 1909.
Stanley Jackson, *The Sassoons*, London, 1968.
Roy Jenkins, *Sir Charles Dilke*, London, 1965.
E. Kennedy, *My Dear Duchess*, London, 1956.
Anita Leslie, *Edwardians in Love*, London, 1972.
Ralph G. Martin, *Jennie*, New York, 1969-1971.
Xavier Paoli, *My Royal Clients*, London, 1911.
Arthur Ponsonby, *Life and Letters of Henry Ponsonby*, London, 1942.
Frederick Ponsonby, *Recollections of Three Reigns*, London, 1951
Joanna Richardson, *Sarah Bernhardt*, London, 1959.
Joanna Richardson, *The Courtesans*, London, 1967.
W. H. Russell, *A Diary in the East during the Tour of the Prince and Princess of Wales*, London, 1869.
W. H. Russell, *The Prince of Wales's Tour*, London, 1877.
Francis Greville, Earl of Warwick, *Memories of Sixty Years*, London, 1917.
Tomahawk, a Saturday Journal of Satire, London, 1867-1870.
La Vie Parisienne, Paris passim.

RADIO TIMES HULTON PICTURE LIBRARY Pages: 10, 13, 16, 18, 38, 39, 46, 51, 53, 62, 68, 69, 72, 74, 77, 80, 82, 84, 89, 90, 97, 98, 104, 105, 117, 119, 120, 122, 124, 134, 137, 148, 149, 152, 153, 155, 156, 157, 160, 161, 170, 171, 174, 177, 178, 184, 185.
INTERPIX Pages: 8, 9, 11, 12, 14, 17, 66, 86, 87, 105, 114, 115, 127, 138, 139, 145, 146, 155, 163, 175, 176, 180, 181, 186.
ILLUSTRATED LONDON NEWS L.E.A. Pages: 20, 42, 43, 54, 58, 60, 66, 121, 140, 159, 162, 172, 183.
MARY EVANS Pages: 19, 22, 23, 30, 36, 41, 107, 158, 173.
BASSANO & VANDYK Pages: 137, 153, 164.
THE BRITISH LIBRARY Pages: 101, 102, 125.
NATIONAL PORTRAIT GALLERY Pages: 35, 122.

Index